A little bit
Asperger?

A little bit Asperger?

Life with my adorable Aspie

Juliet Walke

A little bit Asperger?
Juliet Walke

Published by Greyhound Self-Publishing 2020
Malvern, Worcestershire, United Kingdom.

Printed and bound by Aspect Design
89 Newtown Road, Malvern, Worcs. WR14 1PD
United Kingdom
Tel: 01684 561567
E-mail: allan@aspect-design.net
Website: www.aspect-design.net

All Rights Reserved.

Copyright © 2020 Juliet Walke

Juliet Walke has asserted her moral right
to be identified as the author of this work.

The right of Juliet Walke to be identified as the author
of this work has been asserted in accordance with
Section 77 of the Copyright, Designs and Patents Act 1988.

This book is sold subject to the condition that it shall not, by way of trade or otherwise, be lent, resold, hired out or otherwise circulated without the publisher's prior consent in any form of binding or cover other than that in which it is published and without a similar condition including this condition being imposed on the subsequent purchaser.

A copy of this book has been deposited with the British Library Board

Cover Design Copyright © 2020 Aspect Design
Original photograph Copyright © 2020
ISBN 978-1-909219-65-6

CONTENTS

Introduction	7
Head over heels	11
How could you *do* that?	15
Words, words, words…	24
Goose and Gander…?	33
Cool, Calm and Collector!	44
How do you think that made me feel?	50
What do you expect me to do?	62
I'm all yours	72
Points of Viewing	84
Tread Softly…	95
ACKNOWLEDGEMENTS	107
Recommended Reading	108

INTRODUCTION

I need to make one or two things about this book clear at the outset. It is a very personal story about living with a still beloved (now ex) husband. We were together almost exactly seventeen years, and it was a very interesting journey, to use a cliché. It was only during the last year or so of our shared life that it began to dawn on me that, if he had Asperger Syndrome, which I was only just beginning to learn a fair bit about, it could explain a lot about the way he lived his life that many who knew him found difficult to comprehend or, in some cases, tolerate. Like many adults with AS, Gerry was never diagnosed as having it. (According to Maxine Aston in her excellent book *Aspergers in Love*, at least one in two hundred and fifty people in the UK has Asperger Syndrome, and the number is likely to be higher since so many adults remain undiagnosed. An estimated 68% of the population in the US are somewhere on the Autistic Spectrum, and AS now classes in DSM5 as Autistic Spectrum Disorder 1 – ASD 1).

At a GP visit Gerry insisted on making on impulse, he was asked: "Has it ever affected your work?" When the reply was negative the GP pronounced that he therefore couldn't possibly have it, despite the on-line test indicating a strong tendency in that direction. One professional, who had known him extremely well for many years and had worked a lot with children with AS, at first assured him he didn't have it; but in the light of more recent events now considers that he probably does have 'a diagnosis'. The other, who knew him less well but knows a fair bit of detail from my accounts, is convinced that he has a triple cluster of personality patterns (my term, as I do wish the term 'disorder' could be knocked out of usage), among them Asperger's. This man was a full-time professional in Psychology and has a partner who <u>has</u> been officially diagnosed as having AS.

Another point to make clear is that this is not a book describing the syndrome; there are plenty of books now available, and I shall list a few commendable ones at the end. Every individual Aspie is unique – thank goodness, as that is the glory of human beings! Some who, on reading this book, may recognise themselves or some of their ways described here may be inclined to feel criticised. However, it may be more helpful to think of these descriptions as observations on the way some people act, which is not (neuro-) typical in a majority of the population. My own view is that you can only *criticise* an action or repeating pattern that is within the person's control and over which they have choice. With the AS brain-wiring, what is obvious to many as inappropriate things to say or do is completely unknown territory, and therefore should not attract *criticism*. Nevertheless it may help an Aspie's path through life ('How to win friends and influence people'!) if someone close can gently and kindly point out the probable consequences of certain ways in terms of others' hurt feelings, opposite outcomes to what the Aspie really hopes for, and then – albeit with great effort – (s)he can learn patterns of response more likely to achieve what is desired.

INTRODUCTION

Much detail has been modified to protect privacy, but the essentials and verbatim quotes are all genuine. And now a note to my adored Gerry: If this book ever comes into your hands – and in many ways I hope it doesn't – please try not to see any of the incidents I relate, or descriptions of how you were, as criticism. I know how much it hurts you whenever you feel you are being criticised; and how this has often affected or even destroyed work you revelled in and are, at present anyway, no longer given the opportunity to do. What I recount in this book are loving observations. If they <u>were</u> criticisms, I don't think – writing this three and a half years after you left me – that I would still adore you and long to be back with you as I most surely do. If I had so many criticisms I would not have dearly and devoutly wished for us to be together 'till death us (do) part' – and I truly did; but you chose otherwise. You are unique, extremely talented and oh so lovable! I guess my dearest wish would be for you to feel more at home in this strange world of ours, and to find it easier to put up with us disadvantaged neuro-typical folk. I know you longed for a 'perfect relationship', as it was in your written wish-list of 2011. I would have loved us to make it as nearly perfect as possible, but for my own part, I'm just a mortal with her own wounds. I wish I'd understood, through the years, what it was that contributed to the way you are and I might have responded even more helpfully. In the words of Billy Joel '*I love you just the way you are*'. God bless!

Chapter One

HEAD OVER HEELS

It all began like the most romantic of fairy tales … I guess I know what you may be thinking already: that it soon became a nightmare. But it didn't. The way Gerry used to describe his sudden arrival in my life went something like this: "I crashed in through your front door with a JCB and unloaded tons of love for you." That's just how it felt – though I'm happy to say there was no actual structural damage! – and it was the nicest imaginable kind of shock. A shock to the system it certainly was, however.

Only about six weeks earlier, a very delightful relationship I'd been having with a guy the same age as me ended rather abruptly when he rang from abroad and said he'd had an amazing encounter with a spiritual teacher and was so impressed with this way of life that he planned to move in there forever. He would be settling up his affairs in this country and would come to see me if I wished but would understand if I didn't. Initially I was pretty devastated but figured that if – as I believed – this lovely relationship had been "sent to me" another equally lovely relationship could just as easily come my way. I perhaps hadn't expected it to happen so soon, so suddenly and so romantically, but that was all pretty wonderful.

For someone like me it was most unusual to make such a rash

decision so suddenly. For, though I knew Gerry slightly through friends of his, our first proper meeting was to be a Sunday lunch, which I invited him to at my house. His previous relationship had ended a couple of months earlier and he was just moving into a flat. Between a Friday afternoon phone call and the planned Sunday lunch visit, we had two or three chats on the phone and he also left several answer-phone messages, one of which astounded me when I heard him say: "I think I'm falling in love with you". When he rang on the Saturday evening at about 8:30 p.m. and asked how I was feeling about the next day, he said: "Well I can't wait till tomorrow. Can I come over this evening?" He did, and went home again on the Sunday evening, promising to visit again the next day.

When he rang on the Monday he said: "I have a very important question to ask you when I come over." I thought: "Surely not the question that just sprang into my mind ... but just in case, I think I'll go and buy a bottle of bubbly". Sure enough, he did ask me to marry him and – you might say crazily – I said: "Yes" and had never been so sure of anything in my life. It took no time at all to realise that he had huge amounts of charm and a refreshing and disarming level of honesty. He had told me on the phone, before he ever came over, about all his previous intimate relationships; so common sense might have whispered "Caution" in my ear. I am normally a very level-headed, sensible and often <u>over</u>-cautious individual! I am also pretty intuitive and I actually believe my intuition stood me in good stead on this occasion.

The next few weeks were heady, blissful and great fun and I was convinced that here was a man who was truly loving me the way I'd always needed to be loved. Meeting my children over the Christmas period was of course a bit of a challenge for all concerned. At twenty-one and twenty-three they must have thought I was out of my tiny mind, but were kind enough not to say so. It was a tremendous shock when, late in January, Gerry said that, with huge regret, he needed to break off our engagement. We had got engaged at the end of November and, reluctant to wait until the following May when I had envisaged a wedding with lovely early summer flowers, Gerry had suggested that we should marry on Valentine's Day and have a blessing in the May. I forgot to mention that he and all his chattels had moved in with somewhat indecent haste; so after he had announced his departure his vast collection of LPs, books etc and his enormous quantity of toy soldier – sorry, Wargaming! – paraphernalia were moved out again.

We kept in touch by phone and met occasionally and it eventually came to light that he'd "fallen in love" over the phone again, this time with a woman living overseas. One might imagine a number of friends and relations having good reason to think: "Well what could you expect?" They probably despaired of me, and the friend who had introduced us in the first place was clearly worried about my mental health because I was convinced he would come back to me sooner or later. This he did the following September, having not even been happy to stay for the full 10 day visit that was planned to get to know this other woman properly. "What an incredibly impulsive individual!" you may be thinking. And was the woman who took him back so readily also misguided and reckless?

Clearly the two of us had each had a really rough time in our own way, so I tentatively enquired if he might like to have a few days away with me in the autumn. Just before we went he had sounded me out, saying: "I've been wondering, if I were to ask you again if you would marry me, what would you be likely to say?" I replied: "It's funny you should say that; I've been wondering the same thing. If you were to ask me, and I decided to say yes, I would want the wedding date to be fixed very soon, before you could change your mind again." Having already apologised profusely to me many times for having broken off the engagement and done such a stupid thing, he now reassured me: "There is no way I would ever do that to you again. I promise I will make it up to you." Thus it was that he moved back in: yes, with all his vast collections of possessions again, and we were married as soon as the six weeks' residency requirement was fulfilled. I think it is fair to say that we were both equally blissfully happy and remained so for many years.

Chapter Two

HOW COULD YOU *DO* THAT?

From my slight acquaintance with Gerry before, I knew that he was an unusual man, and I'm sure that was part of the attraction. (I'm an Aquarian, if that means anything to you! – a certain love of unconventionality etc.) One of his long-term acquaintances said to me, when we were first introduced, "Ah! Gerry's one of the last of the true great eccentrics." Gerry himself has said to me more than once: "I know people think I'm weird." I said: "Not weird, just delightfully unusual!" There were a lot of his features that seemed to me contradictory. After just being introduced to somebody if we were out socially, he would say "What a sweet guy!" – as if he knew all there was to know about him. If he liked somebody, he was full of superlatives. However, if we were driving behind someone, who was clearly looking for a turning or a parking space it would be "What a pillock! He shouldn't be on the road." I'd say: "You too will be elderly, with slower reactions, one day!"

The superlatives about me were wonderful to hear; e.g. " You know I worship you, don't you?" I wasn't entirely comfortable with the choice of that word, which I feel belongs to Big G. Having said that, I know that the word 'adore' has a similar root meaning. I guess I didn't stop to think that, if you're placed on a high pedestal by someone, there's only one direction to go eventually.

I soon noticed that Gerry was extremely outspoken about what he thought of someone, or what they were doing, and would voice an opinion – not just without thinking whether or not it was wise to utter it out loud – but seemingly completely oblivious to the probable consequences of doing so. His regular work (of which he had very little in those early months) was as a professional musician. I shall never forget one gig with a small band he loved working with. Admittedly the band-leader's partner had been a bit excruciating to watch and listen to in the first half; but having told the band-leader so in the interval, Gerry seemed surprised that the singer walked off in a huff and he himself was not invited to play with that band leader again for many years! He also, some years later, walked up to another professional solo instrumentalist, who we used to admire and listen to every year at a favourite haunt of ours, and pointed out to him that he was getting a particular chord wrong every time in one of the tunes in his repertoire. I felt mortified and only realised many years later that it's not wise to feel responsible for the way one's partner acts; and if no embarrassment is felt by the person making what seems to be a colossal 'gaffe' the partner would do well to realise that others will make up their own minds about each individual in the duo.

I have great respect for what John Gray writes in *Men are from Mars, Women are from Venus*, especially with regard to what he claims each of the two genders needs from the opposite one. The particular quality that I have most in mind is a man's need for **approval**. In Gerry's case, he had a strong feeling that he'd been considered as the 'black sheep of the family', not often conforming to his mother's hopes and wishes, and therefore feeling a lot of

disapproval from her and – surprise, surprise – from his first wife and his next long-term live-in partner. He didn't need any more from me!

Nevertheless I kept getting surprises about things he did, and would express that in what I thought was a pleasant way, sometimes with a gentle tease or a touch of humour. I well remember his retort if I ever said: "People just don't *do* that!" or "You can't say *that*!" With a big grin he'd reply: "I just did!" Sadly, what he 'just did' sometimes contributed to his losing work or activities that he'd really enjoyed. One college where he worked for a time may not have appreciated his using literally reams of their paper over several terms, printing up articles he personally wanted from the Internet – before we were 'on line' at home – while he waited for me to pick him up when I finished work.

A friend of mine once invited both of us round for Sunday lunch. The two husbands had met briefly a few times, either at concerts where Gerry had been performing, or when he'd been asked to bring his Wargaming soldiers along to a charity event they organised. The lunch invitation was the first visit to their home, which was a huge house they shared with another couple and where they offered Bed and Breakfast accommodation. While our host was taking my coat in the hall, Gerry walked straight into what he presumed was their Sitting Room, out the other end of it into a guest dining area, and then re-appeared with a book about another hobby that interested him, only to learn that the book belonged to the other man who lived there. It wouldn't have occurred to him to ask: "Shall I go in?" at the door, let alone: "Is it alright if I look at the books on the shelves I can see in the next room?" Come to think of it, wherever we went, he would tend to act as if he owned the place!

I've used the word 'adorable' in the sub-title of this book because I always have adored this man from our first proper conversation, and always will. Others find him extremely likable in many ways, but haven't always happily accepted some of his odder ways in the long term. I'm very fortunate that my children and partners, and my closest friends, were always welcoming to us both. However, once I was on my own again, some interesting revelations came out as to how some of them had reacted to things they had seen him do, or heard him say. A couple who offered us holidays in their home many times (starting when Gerry suddenly lost the only full-time work he had, for one year of our seventeen years of life together) each had their own response to how he was. The wife said to me: "If you didn't know Gerry you'd sometimes think he was being rude." The husband perhaps put it a bit less kindly: "As long as we were sitting in the sun lounge all listening to him talking about his musical work or his hobby, fine! But the minute anyone else wanted to talk about something it was '*I'm out of here, straight into the lounge to put the television on*', without so much as a 'by your leave'!"

We all know that members of the male sex have a reputation for hogging the TV remote control – though not always justly! Gerry never consulted any guests we had staying over, if or what they might want to view; and yet if we stayed in other people's homes he would always decide when and what to watch. My mouth must have dropped open in astonishment the first time he did the latter. In our own home I would probably ask the guests if there was anything *they* would like to watch. It was the way I'd been brought up, to try and consider what other people's preferences might be if it involved doing something, going somewhere or choosing programmes to listen to or watch. Another known-to-be Aspie friend I went to stay with once or twice *played the part* of the charming host. On my first evening he said: "Now, what would you like to do tomorrow?" – and then gave me three options to consider. I said they all sounded good, but stated my clear preference, with enthusiastic reasons. At breakfast the next morning he announced: "Instead of going to (where I'd chosen) I thought we'd do such-and-such." This was a possibility that hadn't even been mentioned the night before, and stated in a tone of voice that indicated it was not up for debate!

That episode was a bit like the last time Gerry and I spent our wedding anniversary weekend in our romantic honeymoon village. When he'd filled up the car with diesel in the nearby town, he'd been disappointed to find that the garage car-wash was out of action; so he said: "If you don't mind, Cookie (his pet name for me), we'll go over to the next town (six miles away) to use the car-wash there. Is that alright?" I said that I'd rather not, pointing out that not only were we going to that town the following day in any case and could do it then, but I was looking forward to our planned walk in the woods near the hotel (we always both enjoyed that every year) and it would be getting too dark by the time we'd been to the other town, washed the car by hand and come back. My wishes were ignored, despite the two phrases that appeared to want to take them into account, and I was prepared to take the dimly-lit walk in the woods on my own, out of sheer frustration, on our return to base. Gerry asked if it was alright to come with me and I agreed; but there was certainly an atmosphere of tension instead of the carefree pleasure that those walks usually offered. That was the first time I felt Gerry and I had had a 'row', in sixteen years! – and over such a trivial thing.

Choice of listening was also a bit of an issue on our long car journeys. A friend I know who's married to an Aspie says he never wants to talk in the car, however long the journey. Another friend who has an Aspie son says they had to forget having any say in what viewing or listening was chosen. This can be very frustrating if one feels one has to give in to it. I tried various ways to try to resolve this when we were travelling. My first suggestion was: " Could we please take it in turns an hour at a time to choose whether and what to listen to?" I think the agreement to do this was given rather grudgingly, and if I chose classical music for a while (he was classically trained at Music College) I would switch off quickly if the composer whose music he doesn't like came on. It worked quite well if we took tapes of light music we both like; and I was happy with some Radio 4 programmes. But I didn't feel that heavy subjects put us in a carefree leisurely mood, and learned early on that it was best not to converse at all for the first half-hour or so, until Gerry had begun to relax into the holiday spirit. With hindsight, although it was totally hidden from view, I think there was a huge insecurity about leaving behind the familiar surroundings, even when we were headed for the parts of the country that he loved best.

For this reason, choosing holiday destinations needed some care. I had grown up in the Midlands, and family holidays for me were often down in Dorset, so I liked nothing better than to return there and go to some of the quieter beaches I knew well – though not for sun-worshipping or lounging around. Gerry grew up in the North of England, and it was Scotland that he always longed to return to on holiday, as he had done in childhood. Fortunately I love Scotland too, and never tired of it; so realising that all but one of our holidays in various parts of Dorset had resulted in Gerry being somewhat morose for all or part of it, I gave in graciously and realised that holidays together would be much more enjoyable if we always went to shared favourite spots. For an occasional Dorset 'fix' I would go on my own for a few days' B & B. I'm grateful that we had so many super trips to the far north, not least because his previous partner had complained to a friend that they never went away anywhere. On recalling this comment, he would often laugh to me and say "Don't we have a fabulous time, Cookie?" It's true that, living in a Derbyshire spa town we were surrounded by beautiful countryside, but it's still good to have a change of scene with mini-breaks now and then. For what turned out to be the final summer holiday before he left me, I wondered if he might be more content if <u>he</u> chose all the detail. Little did I suspect that this would add greatly to his stress. After all, a huge part of his working life was spent ferreting out information on line, and locating resources that he needed in connection with his journalism. When I asked how he'd got on, he said it was hopeless; he couldn't find anything. I enquired – diplomatically I think – how he'd set about it. He replied that he'd typed into the search engine box: "Cheap holidays UK", but this had got him no satisfactory results. I remarked that I would be quite happy to go again to an area where we'd been before, and it might be a good idea if he made that a starting point.

One particular Dorset holiday proved that part of his reluctance was an almost phobic reaction to narrow lanes with high hedges. When I did a further professional training in 2009, more on the counselling side, we were encouraged to consider in depth how to be 'true to ourselves'. As I regularly did these exercises to go deeply into this, I realised with full force that – almost – my very survival depended on having some time near the sea, preferably for at least a few days twice a year. I was overjoyed when I discovered a tiny little cottage that was affordable to rent, despite our fairly modest incomes, in my favourite area from childhood holidays and, with Gerry's agreement, I booked it for the February half-term week. My excitement was enormous, not just for that particular week of bliss, but because it seemed like the start of a regular pattern of something I'd been yearning for without fully realising it. Better still, an alternative centre (we're both quite alternative people!) with a lovely restaurant was able to take my last-minute booking for a Valentine's Night dinner. Imagine the wretchedness of Valentine's Night with your beloved who's looking utterly miserable, when other couples are particularly close and blissed-out, all because – as I thought at the time – the guest house was so difficult to find in the dark and involved a journey along narrow lanes for five out of the eight miles. Needless to say we were never able to return to the sweet little cottage for further holidays.

A curious thing used to occur, which later made sense to me when I understood AS better. Often a pure diary oversight or car breakdown would cut short our planned times away and it happened far too many times to be pure coincidence. Since I believe that we can unconsciously sabotage things if we have very strong feelings around an issue, I am convinced that – though a great time was always had in his preferred holiday venues, and we would be very close at those times – nevertheless he found holidays quite anxiety-making; although, as I wrote earlier, this was quite well concealed.

Chapter Three

WORDS, WORDS, WORDS…
or: "When I say plums, surely you know I mean pears!"

Gerry has a tremendous talent with words. When very young he had a reading age well in advance of his years, and his creative writing had rated special mention from his teachers: sometimes for inappropriate themes for one of such tender years! So gifted was his use of language that a large part of his paid work through many years was technical journalism, presented in a very readable style.

All that was when he was *writing*, and when the subject had no emotional content whatever. When he was speaking, again he was very articulate on all the special subjects about which he was so knowledgeable, and his listeners seemed to find this interesting – for a certain length of time; though he never picked up the cues of waning interest or even boredom that I could sometimes read on their faces. These topics could be the music for which he did his professional training (but a much broader and more eclectic mix than he had covered at Music College) or the Wargaming hobby that so fascinated him. His memory for the exact year things happened, where and at what price things had been bought, not to mention the phenomenally long list of people's telephone numbers that he had by heart, were quite astounding. The latter is of course more to do with memory than words. Nevertheless it is indicative of an unusual capability for the storing, cataloguing and recall of factual material.

When it came to the *heard* word, however, it was a different thing entirely. I can guess what many women reading this next section are likely to remark, something along the lines of: "Oh, all men are like that. They never listen properly. They often get the wrong end of the stick – and they never can find things. That's nothing to do with Asperger's." One retired social worker I know well said airily to me: "Oh well, they say that Asperger's is just like being a man, only more so. After all, we're all somewhere on the (autistic) spectrum." I think I would add: "We're all on various kinds of spectrum, and it's only by observing hundreds of instances of a phenomenon that it finally dawns that there is a detectable pattern here that probably means something particular". The reader will doubtless be relieved to learn that I only plan to give one or two examples of these, not hundreds! What I'm thinking of here is times when Gerry would call out something like: "Cookie, do you know where my green jumper is?" and I'd reply: "It's in the bottom of the chest of drawers." I'd hear a few bangs and thuds, then: "It isn't; I've looked." I'd ask if he wanted me to come up and help find it, and there he'd be peering into the bottom of the *wardrobe*. I was going to write that, if speaking and referring to pieces of furniture, he'd always normally use the right word. Then I remembered that on one occasion much later, when flustered, he referred to the chaise longue – which he'd named correctly many times – as 'the recliner chair'. To quote one of his own favourite quips: "Close, but no cigar"!

Similarly, if we were preparing a meal in the kitchen, he would get very muddled between what we called the 'ice box' (below the fridge compartment) in the kitchen and the freezer, which was kept in a utility room just beyond the kitchen. The whole reason we decided to call the first one the 'ice box' was because he had just found it too confusing to distinguish between the 'chest freezer' (out the back) and the freezer part of the fridge/freezer. I also found that, if instructions had to be given verbally, only one matter should be dealt with at a time. Similarly, if Gerry was on his way out of the door and called out: "Do we need anything from the shop?", two was the maximum number of items to be retained. If it was three, only the last two would be remembered.

Because I gradually realised there was a need to explain things very carefully in order to avoid misunderstanding, I tried to tread a very fine line between giving enough information and explanation for clarity (also so that it 'sank in'), and over-complicating matters. When, after very many years, tensions started to develop between us, my careful attempts to communicate things clearly were dubbed 'patronising'. Two notable occasions stick in my mind, when – despite careful explanations of my reasons for requesting a particular way of doing things – Gerry over-ruled that with disastrous consequences. The first was the run-up to one Christmas Eve, when we had presents to deliver to a friend and a family of relatives in another town. Earlier in the day we'd met a different friend for lunch and exchange of presents, walking around a pleasant little place mid-way between where she lived and where we lived. The other deliveries were on our way home and as we headed there I said to Gerry, who was driving: "I know we'll be passing (the road where the relatives lived) and will have to double back half a mile, but we need to take Pam's present to the shop where she works before her finish time, because it's impossible to park anywhere near her house and I've just about reached the limit of my walking capacity today."

I have a minor spinal injury which limits the amount of walking I can do in a given day. If I ignore the early warning signs, very frequent excruciating spasms are set off and usually last ten days or so, with no medication or procedure ever having been found to ease them.

Without further discussion Gerry proceeded to the relatives' house, and when we had handed over their presents he insisted on going to Pam's place of work anyway, saying: "I expect she'll still be there." She wasn't (what a surprise that she knew her own finish time at work better than Gerry did!!) and so we had the whole rigmarole of parking a long way from Pam's house and having to walk along icy pavements to reach her. Whilst I'm sure she wouldn't have minded having my present to her a bit late, she *would* have minded that we hadn't received the Christmas Pud she always insisted on making for us in time. My back spasms started that evening, making the rest of Christmas rather tricky. I can accept that my own muscle tension from frustration contributed to that episode, but – guess what – I'm human, and have my limitations!

The other occasion was quite similar. I had a long-standing arrangement to meet another friend for lunch in a town at a half-way point between us, about 10 miles away. Gerry fancied coming along for the ride as it would give him the opportunity to look round a different selection of his beloved charity shops. He also helpfully added that, instead of joining us in a café for lunch as we were happy for him to do, he'd use that time to do the big shop that was needed for a special event the next day, getting himself a snack in the store cafeteria. I thanked him and said that would be absolutely brilliant, saving time and energy for the food preparation that I needed to do that evening and next morning for the event. When we met up and I couldn't see the shopping in the car he said cheerily: "No, I decided we'd do it together in the supermarket we pass on the way home. I didn't want to get any of the shopping wrong." I'm afraid the end result was the same as the pre-Christmas episode the other time!

It is generally understood that, with high-functioning autism, dealing with emotions is much more of a challenge than for the average neuro-typical individual. (But please note the word 'individual', as we are all that, and there is so much variation in responses and manifestations.) Needless to say, *talking about feelings* is especially challenging. I shall never forget a period of a couple of weeks (after we'd been married for about five or six years) when I was getting 'the silent treatment' from Gerry, which was very unusual. I kept wondering "What have I done wrong?" When I felt I'd given long enough for whatever was bugging him to wear off, and was still none the wiser, I gently asked: "You don't seem very happy lately. Have I done something to upset you?" He replied: "Well, I can't seem to do anything right lately. You're always picking on me." (Over time it became abundantly clear that he construed as criticism many, many remarks or comments which were nothing of the kind, and this applied to feedback from other people as well as from me, and in several cases led to loss of work that he'd loved doing.) On this occasion I was shocked and horrified, as I hadn't seen that. I said: "I'm sorry if that's the case. Let me have a think for a while and then perhaps we could talk about it … Maybe this evening?" He agreed and we did.

As I reflected for an hour or so, I could recall coming in several times from a long hard day seeing patients in a clinic 22 miles away (I'm a physiotherapist), having done grocery shopping in my lunch hour and, once home, expressing displeasure that Gerry had left a huge pile of dirty dishes in the kitchen, having watched science fiction videos for most of the day. When we had our 'couple talk' I admitted to this and asked if there were any other ways he'd felt 'picked on'. He said there weren't, and I apologised if my tone of voice had been carping lately, and tried to excuse myself by saying that I put it down to my very high anxiety levels. He asked what on earth I was worried about, and I said: "You losing your full-time job." It was the only full-time job he'd had since we'd been together, and in fact there never was another throughout the 17 years. It had lasted only one year, but during that wonderful year we were able to afford to do more or less what we wanted for the first time; for example have five or six B & B weekends away, as well as a week's summer holiday and our usual anniversary long weekend.

Gerry's remark that he'd had no idea that I'd been worried (and still couldn't see any valid reason for it) prompted me to suggest that it might be good if we set up regular short 'couple meetings', just for a limited time period, when we each would take turns to say how we were feeling at the time – about our work life, married life, and anything else that was very much on our minds. We'd also make notes about what the other said, after 'mirroring' it back to each other so that both of us felt heard and understood. Then we'd decide if we needed to take any action to improve anything and would set the interval for the next meeting, if we wanted another. We always began by lighting a candle, turning to each other on the sofa and holding hands quietly for a few minutes before we began, to reach some stillness and remind ourselves how much our togetherness meant. This beneficial practice fell away during the last few years before he left me, with the result that – when things were really falling apart – he said: "I didn't realise you weren't completely happy."

Gerry is such an adoring person that he had never had any difficulty expressing his love, both in words and by touch. I am so very, very fortunate and blessed to have had that gift from him for a good fifteen years, with the tactile part of our relationship diminishing just a little after the first five or so. You may laugh at this, but part of the reason seemed to be that, once we had a cat, instead of loving to stroke my feet, which Gerry had always invited me to rest on his lap as we watched TV, he would stroke the cat instead!

It's very much in my nature to digress: what I was really leading up to was Gerry's struggle to find the right words when feeling emotional.

When my newest grandson was little my son had asked me if I would like to accompany the three of them for a week's holiday in Spain. Gerry had to work with the various choirs he was conducting by then and would have hated being there with us in a confined space without his computer and with a need to be outdoors most of the time, but he told me he was more than happy for me to go with them. When it came to the moment of my departure he stood on our doorstep with a face like a sad little boy's and simply said: "This doesn't feel right!" There were other times when we spent a few days away from each other, either because of a school band tour or other musical commitments of his, or for my Family History trips of a night or two, which had previously bored him somewhat, leading him to opt out. I hated being away from him, but realised that it can bring freshness into relationships if there are separate activities to tell each other about (more about that in Chapter 5). Among all those occasions, I don't think he ever said: "I shall miss you!" Or, on my return: "I've missed you."

The other aspect of using words which, with hindsight, I now realise Gerry found daunting was 'small talk'. Three or four times a year we would attend a Community Lunch, where initially I knew the people much better than he did. But he's not in the least shy, always joined the event of his own volition, and was happy to sit next to whoever it turned out to be. Often I'd be helping to serve, so would be to-ing and fro-ing, aware of his conversations with his neighbour, which were usually quite lengthy and on the topic of his musical activities. I can never recall seeing Gerry even once listening to someone else talking, except to pals at one of their Wargaming Conventions. At the Community Lunches, he was always the first to finish his food – despite chattering away – and I became the envy of female friends there, because he would leap up and go to the kitchen to run water for the washing up, return to collect empty plates (not enquiring if anyone wanted second helpings!), then whisk them off and wash everything in sight. Other women there assumed he did the same with alacrity at home, which was far from the truth!

The exception was that, from time to time if we had friends round for dinner, as soon as he had finished his main course, he would rush to the kitchen and start washing up, a few feet away from us, regardless of how much food the guests still had on their plates. Once this had happened a couple of times, I quietly explained before our next dinner party that – though it was lovely of him to do lots of the clearing up, I'd much prefer it if we both relaxed with and chatted to the people we'd invited, preferably leaving the washing up till after they'd gone, or even the next morning; but certainly not doing it between courses, which seemed to have the effect of making guests feel they had better hurry up! This explanation was to no avail, and over time I realised how utterly uncomfortable it was for Gerry to sit amidst conversation when he wasn't the focal point, preferably the speaker, and that he not only wasn't interested in anything someone else might want to talk to *him* about; he had no clue whatsoever about how a person can encourage a guest to talk rather than just be talked at. This made for some very awkward situations, as referred to earlier, in Chapter Two. Really the whole matter of Reciprocity was a mystery to him, so I'd like to explore that in the next chapter.

Chapter Four

GOOSE AND GANDER…?

This is going to be a tricky chapter for me. I've done lots and lots of thinking around it, because it could so easily end up sounding like a 'good guy / bad guy' comparison. That's not at all what I intend. It isn't like that. There are various reasons for my writing this book. One is to try and give myself some meaning after mayhem, I suppose a sort of writing therapy amidst huge heartache. Another is the chance that one or two people who read it may be helped, either from a sense of "Wow! I didn't know that anyone else had that kind of experience / feeling. I feel a bit better for knowing that." Ultimately, too, I hope that a few crumbs of 'hindsight wisdom' that I may be able to drop could perhaps save a similar situation and lead to a happier outcome for both parties. But if what follows sounds like criticism, please remember the sub-title of the book. I adored Gerry from the moment he walked through my door, adored him (except perhaps for a sum total of an hour or two) throughout the seventeen years we lived together; I still do, and I'm certain I always will. What's different now is that I can refute the adjective 'selfish', which a handful of people who've known him for decades use to describe Gerry, because I believe I now have a full understanding of why being 'considerate of other people's feelings' is so very difficult for him to achieve.

It's simply because his brainwave patterns just do not allow him to enter through imagination into how other people are likely to respond to things he does and says.

What this chapter is mainly about is *Reciprocity*. I love words in all sorts of ways and I like the sound of this one. But, oh my! – how my hopes were disappointed as the years went by, and I found that most of the time it just wasn't there in our relationship. You may have heard the old joke about the couple many years ago who were interviewed on their Golden Wedding. (Remember how old such people used to look in the local newspaper photos? – not any more. Maybe that's because I'm seventy as I write this!) Anyway, the journalist asked the husband what he thought was the reason for their long and happy marriage. He smiled and replied: "Give and take. She gives, and I take." Gerry was always absolutely wonderful at expressing appreciation of anything I did that was a benefit for him, especially the meals I cooked. For his own part, he was apt to fish for compliments, and the one that amused me most was when I used to come in from a long day's work, those times when he <u>had</u> done something in the kitchen. He would draw my attention and say: "Did you see I've done the washing-up?" I would get the message and say: "Yes, thanks very much!" I don't remember a single occasion when I got thanks for the same thing. Clearly, despite his being in many ways a 'New Age Man', washing-up was <u>my</u> responsibility, so if he relieved me of it from time to time, it merited special thanks!

Among his favourite meals I cooked were a melt-in-the-mouth pork and apple casserole, and rhubarb crumble, welcome any time as far as he was concerned. If he ate yoghurt, it was the rhubarb one day after day after day. I left curry cooking to him as the expert. In fact it was months before I admitted to him that I'd never ever liked curry, except a mild korma. Nevertheless, curry spices (which he always endearingly called herbs) ended up in all sorts of dishes where you wouldn't expect them, like my beloved cauliflower cheese! When I made the toast for lunch I always remembered to leave Gerry's pieces under the grill for quite a bit longer than mine, to make it the way he liked it. Unfortunately, despite a good many patient reminders, the converse did not apply and I often had to resort to scraping my slice if he was griller-in-chief that day.

I know that every couple finds their own style. Some – and I know a couple of examples who seem very happy with this – seem to live 'in each other's pockets', hardly ever going anywhere or doing anything independently in their leisure time. If that suits, it's fine. At the other extreme some couples rarely seem to do anything together, and observers are left wondering what it is that keeps them together. Again, it's nobody's business but theirs and it can work well for years if both parties are content with that lifestyle. When Gerry and I first got together I had been living on my own for six-and-a-half years, and had become reasonably self-sufficient, though looking forward to the companionship of a new life-sharing relationship if that came along. I was astonished and delighted that Gerry was eager for so much togetherness. The fact that he barely left my side in the early months might have irritated some, but for me it was an indication of how much he adored me, and that at last he'd found 'the right one'. I was totally convinced of the latter. If I had a hair appointment, he wanted to drive me to the hairdresser's (much earlier than I would normally have gone, as it was only just up the road!). If we were in town shopping in several different places and the final call was at the Newsagent's at the bottom of our road, he'd prefer me to get out of the car and go in with him, even if he was just picking up his Miniature Wargaming magazine. This was not in any way because he appeared to lack the confidence to do anything on his own. To most people he appears to have an *excess* of self-confidence, and definitely has 'the gift of the gab' when talking to people like shop-keepers and hotel staff – within the parameters mentioned in the previous chapter.

As far as his musical engagements were concerned, he liked me to go along to all the folk gigs where he was playing guitar. I would always say: "Is it open to the public?" and he would say that it was, whether or not he'd checked with the person who'd engaged him. I remember several occasions when I tried to make myself as invisible as possible at someone's Silver Wedding do, 50th Birthday or some such. It was particularly embarrassing if food was laid on for the band. Naturally, no-one else in the band brought a partner along! I remember a regular monthly gig in a restaurant where, from time to time, I felt morally obliged to order something to eat as I was taking up space on a busy evening. On those occasions I would probably have to spend nearly as much (on just a starter!) as Gerry earned for playing. After ten or so years, when he was conducting his main Ladies' Choir at several concerts a year, I would also gladly be in the audience, keeping a low profile so that he could concentrate on this work that gave him so much joy. I loved watching him at work in these ways, even though the folk gigs wouldn't have been my choice if I'd never met him.

In the first year or two, Gerry was eager and willing to come along to any events where I was doing a talk, or running a stand about my work as a Physiotherapist, and also to attend AGMs with interesting speakers at the Health Centre, which was my main place of work. He would also say how proud he was of my work. This support for <u>my</u> spheres of work and interest soon wore off, however. If I invited him to come along with me I always left him free to choose (no emotional blackmail!); but if he did so it often seemed grudgingly. When it came to the miniature Wargaming exhibitions or conventions (I forget exactly what they called them) he was really keen for me to come along; in fact would have been devastated if I hadn't. I needed endless patience, not just for the long days at the halls where the aficionados were doing their thing, but for the evenings when, at the B&B where other fans were staying, or the pub where we all had an evening meal, the talk would be exclusively about their hobby, naturally enough, and I became the invisible woman!

When it came to <u>my</u> hobby, however, Gerry found it well-nigh impossible to be gracious about it. I made the Family History trips very short (two or three days maximum), and ensured that the ones where I invited him to come along with me were in places where there was lots to interest him: the sort of museums he loved, plenty of charity shops and second-hand bookshops he could browse in to his heart's content, a meet-up for lunch and a lovely meal out in the evenings. I also refrained from saying too much about my research discoveries, keeping watch for his eyes beginning to glaze over so that we could swiftly change to another subject. One drizzly Sunday afternoon we parked near the gateway to a village churchyard. I didn't hold out much hope of finding any ancestral headstones, since I knew my folk of that era had only been agricultural labourers, but I wanted to look anyway. I left Gerry sitting in the car reading a paperback, then after a few minutes dashed back excitedly, saying: "I've found it! – my great-great grandfather's grave. He was a Churchwarden, so they gave him a headstone." He looked up briefly from his book, said: "Jolly good!" and continued reading. How I would have loved him to say: "Do you want me to come and see it?" I later learned that he couldn't stand any kind of interruption, even if it was the kind offer of a drink in his work-room when he was long overdue for one. However, taking care of this for him must have done him a favour, as a few months after he left he had excruciating pain from a kidney stone, and the doctor evidently told him he hadn't been drinking enough.

My long days at the Clinic, twenty two miles from where we lived, were exhausting. I would usually see about fourteen patients a day for half-an-hour each and, as I mentioned earlier, I'd use most of my lunch hour to do the grocery shopping as there was a large supermarket just across the road. I explained nicely to Gerry several times that, the two nights each week before those really heavy days, I needed at least seven hours' good sleep, so if he wanted to stay up very late watching television, would he please come up very quietly and not put a big light on. Unfortunately, any time I was woken after the first half to one hour of sleep it would always take me around an hour-and-a-half to get back off again, as I suppose the edge had been taken off my tiredness by then. Time and time again this pleasantly-put request would be completely ignored. Fast-forward to a few years later, when Gerry had that year of full-time work teaching at a college, and on those nights he'd announce at 10 p.m.: "We need to go up now, Cookie." And he didn't want me to read in bed because I would need the light on. Once that job came to an end... Yes! You've guessed correctly; he had no inkling of why I needed my sleep before the distant Clinic days! Love him!

Many of these examples may appear trivial. But if we spend many years with a partner, it often seems that the little things mount up and may become increasingly difficult to live with. One example where Gerry found a reciprocal attitude puzzling (to say the least) ended up as a real problem. When my son in Leicestershire said he and his wife wondered if I'd be willing to go over there and look after their little boy for one day every other week, I was delighted. My daughter-in-law Ann wanted to go back to work part-time and her mother was willing to do the 'Nanny Day' the alternate week, and Gerry was fine with that. It seemed perfect that I was needed for Tuesdays, as that was Gerry's busiest day with work in a school, private pupils and - from early evening - his weekly rehearsal with one of the Ladies' Choirs he conducted. He would hardly notice I wasn't there! From the Derbyshire spa town where we lived I just needed to drive over to the M1 and nip down a few junctions and I was soon there, taking about an hour-and-three-quarters on a good run. It meant an early start, but for quality time with my grandson it was worth it. We all agreed I'd stay overnight each time, as the early drive and the non-stop childcare day left me pretty tired at the end of it.

This arrangement went on for a couple of years and everything seemed to be fine. Then I began to feel very unwelcome each time I returned home. I used to drive back on those Wednesdays, trying to time it so that I could at least wave to Gerry as our cars passed, with him on his way to a one-hour school-teaching assignment in our town. This meant we'd have lunch together at home a bit later than usual. I remember how many, many times, as I drove back up the motorway, I would think: "I'm so lucky. Every time I go down the motorway I'm really looking forward to seeing my family, and every time I drive back up I'm excited about seeing Gerry again!" When the cool atmosphere on my return had continued for quite a few weeks, I asked if we could explore it together. Gerry's first comment was that, lately, he'd felt that we hadn't 'connected' each time I'd come back home. We set aside time to talk about it in more detail, and I discovered that what he meant by that was not at all what I'd imagined it to mean, namely something like my not taking enough notice of him. Yet after my fortnightly 24-hour absences I always wanted to spend as much time solely devoted to him and us as he wanted.

When he began to explain what this 'not connecting' felt like to him it went something like this: "While you're away I'm just nice and quiet by myself, thinking my own thoughts; then you come in all bubbly and start talking to me about what you did with Jack and what he said and where you went and who else you met. Well, I don't know these people, and I haven't been to many of these places, so I don't know what you're talking about" (and therefore I don't want to hear it!). I said that now I knew how that felt for him, I would try to just be fairly quiet for the first few hours back and let him get used to my being there again, and also keep conversation about my time away to the minimum. I also felt I should ask him whether being 'nice and quiet here by myself' was a way he was thinking he'd rather live in the long term, to which he replied: "No, of course not!"

I should perhaps add that I didn't make a habit of talking endlessly to Gerry in the normal way of things. I learned pretty early on in our life together that he needed frequent and longish amounts of solitude. For example, I was shocked the first time he went up for a bath and was gone two hours. Although he had a couple of rooms all to himself in the house, the bath was very much a sacred retreat, I think. Conversation opportunities were also very limited by the fact that, as soon as he left his home workplace and came downstairs he would switch on the television, and if nothing on any channel appealed, he would choose a video. This was, of course, quite a contrast to the early months together, when he hardly left my side, and would say to me, especially when we were in bed at night: "What are you thinking?" At that time he wanted to share in every single thing about me and my life. Naturally the first few months of living with someone are bound to be very different from the more measured pattern that emerges over time. With hindsight I wonder if, though he said he enjoyed twenty-four hours of solitude, he also at some level felt abandoned by me one day a fortnight, since he always seemed a bit withdrawn and insecure when I was with my children and grandchildren, whether in their home or ours. I think Gerry experienced a lot of ambivalence about company / no company. I've come across people who want company at home, but in the next room. That sounds about right for Gerry much of the time.

Having listened and tried to understand why he was finding my home-comings difficult, I then asked if I could point out to him that he also often came in bubbling over with things he wanted to tell me. This was usually after he'd given a private pupil a lesson which had gone particularly well and he felt the student was making exceptional progress. A typical comment would be: "Though I say it myself, I think I'm getting rather good at this!" The same thing would happen after an especially good rehearsal with one of the choirs. Appreciation, affirmation and 'positive strokes' were things he craved in huge amounts, partly – I think – because of having been convinced he'd been 'the black sheep of the family' as he grew up. (As I mentioned earlier, he felt this was how his family of origin had labelled him, and he used that expression a number of times as he talked about his parents and siblings, and how he'd never really felt any connection with them.) I gently explained that I loved hearing him talk in this way about the things that are dear to his heart and give him pleasure as, for me, that is part of what my loving him means. I too might not know the people he was talking about at all, or the place where he'd just been on a gig, but I was still interested. He thanked me for showing him this part of the picture of our life together, as it was something he hadn't realised. I guess that later he may have perceived this as a criticism, that he didn't feel or show any corresponding interest in *my* independent activities. However, I was simply trying to point out that we were both doing similar things, that I saw that as part of married life, but that I would try to give consideration to the differences in what he needed from me and the things he could not easily tolerate. At this time no-one who knew Gerry well had considered the possibility of mild Asperger Syndrome having an effect.

Turning over in my mind the ways I, apparently, became a 'bad wife' – though he never used that term, even in the divorce petition – I've spotted something that could be thought of as *reverse reciprocity*. The allegation I'm thinking of was: "…and you've <u>always</u> criticised my driving." In reality, I'd given a gentle reminder about 30 m.p.h. restricted areas in case he hadn't noticed. I knew he'd be devastated if he collided with someone's beloved cat or dog. I also sometimes couldn't avoid a sharp intake of breath at highly dangerous overtakes at times when he was in a bad space emotionally (though I never grabbed the steering wheel, as his first wife had apparently done on one occasion!) What Gerry has cheerfully forgotten are the countless times at junctions when he'd said to me: "You could have gone then!"; or given sharp-toned directions for parking between cars at the kerbside near our home.

Ah well: selective memory is by no means the exclusive preserve of Aspies!

Chapter Five

COOL, CALM AND COLLECTOR!

When Gerry, aged 42, suddenly moved in with me, his belongings filled a small van, and we later hired another van to transport the technical equipment we managed to buy from his previous partner. It was just as well that there were two small rooms in my house that I could put at his disposal once my tenant's six-month lease expired. Even so – as when anyone new moves in – a lot of my own belongings had to be pushed into distant corners so that the space I'd occupied alone could become 'our home'. Gerry had never owned or had any stake in a property. It was not surprising that, as a musician, he owned hundreds of vinyl LPs. These sat in our sitting/dining room on utilitarian shelves he brought with him, chipboard on a metal frame. Much as I love music (though with not quite the same eclectic taste as his) I confess I found this a bit of an eyesore for many years until I eventually found a sideboard that met with his approval and could put them out of sight. I wouldn't have minded so much seeing them all on permanent display if they had been played quite frequently, but they very rarely were. As I explained earlier, the screen in the corner dominated.

For the first many months Gerry's viewing was almost exclusively science fiction videos. He explained to me that the reason he had BetaMax as well as VHS recorders and recordings was that those in the know found the quality of the former much better than the latter. I still couldn't quite follow why recordings of identical episodes needed to be kept in both formats. Still more puzzling was the way that recordings taken off the TV still had to be kept, even when the commercial versions had been obtained from charity shops. But then at that stage I knew nothing whatever about inveterate collectors! I can be a bit of a hoarder of precious memorabilia, but that's not quite the same thing. In the years to come DVDs of the same episodes and series were obtained. For some this would have meant a welcome freeing-up of space; but not for Gerry, as he needed multiple copies of the same things. It got to the point (I once secretly calculated!) where, even if he'd done nothing during his waking hours other than view his DVDs and videos there may well not have been enough life left to do so. I expect I'm exaggerating, but hey, a sense of humour is a great support.

When it came to the hobby magazines, every monthly issue of sets of *Wargame Digest, Meccano Magazine* and *The Courier* had been kept from the time of their first to latest publication. I know that Victorian houses are pretty solidly built, but I became a bit concerned about the vertical mass of these bearing down on the floor joists of the double guest-room on the second floor of the house, especially as our bedroom was directly below it. I asked Gerry if, as we were about to buy a new bed anyway, we could get a king-size pine bed that the magazines could be stored under, with the colossal weight distributed a bit more evenly. Once he'd agreed I began collecting banana boxes every time I went to the supermarket. They were strong and sturdy, with handle-slots for pulling them out from under the bed, and the perfect size to take two piles of magazines side by side. You may be able to guess who carried out the transfer. I didn't complain, because whenever a change at home was something I requested I was willing to take the responsibility for making it. Another of Gerry's traits was that he was willing and eager to put energy and effort into anything that was an idea of his own, but often quite reluctant if it wasn't. I labelled the box-ends carefully with the dates of the magazines each contained. I think you'd call it a labour of love, and I certainly felt a sense of relief and satisfaction when it was complete. However, as time went on I also felt a bit guilty, as if I'd spoilt his fun. While the magazines were all up at the top of the house Gerry took one or two to read in the loo quite frequently, but once I'd moved them it seemed he would only pick one out if he wanted to look up some specific facts and information. For this he had a superb memory for which issue had dealt with a particular topic. It was as if he carried the index in his brain.

Every time a part-work was advertised on the television I used to devoutly hope that he wouldn't subscribe beyond the first cheaper introductory offer. The collection of magazines and crystal specimens that he already owned when he arrived also lay untouched for years and years, until the happy day when one of his students expressed an interest in the larger crystals that were displayed in various places in the house. It was agreed that Gerry would sell the boy the small specimens with the magazines that explained all about them and a little space was reclaimed – for a short while! For his main hobby of Wargaming he naturally kept adding more stock (I learned not to insult by referring to 'toy soldiers'!) and he could use his magnifying glass to paint the new arrivals. An area of about eight cubic metres, under the sloping ceiling in the double guest room, housed all the equipment needed for this, and I would help to carry it down the two flights of stairs and load it into the car whenever he was attending an exhibition as a participant. Apparently I was often the envy, or rather Gerry was, of pals of his whose wives or partners deplored the hobby, complained frequently about it and would never have dreamt of keeping their fellow company on those occasions. A wry footnote to these mentions of where the hobby items were stored: many years later, when trying to explain a few reasons why he'd fallen out of love with me by then, he made a comment that I wouldn't let him keep his Wargaming boards set up all the time because I'd said it was the double guest room and not just his hobby den. (It was, and his own friends and relations had the benefit of staying there, not just mine!) He said he'd forgotten, until I reminded him, about the several years when I would put the guest bed back as stowaway singles, one under the other right against the wall, after visitors departed, thus leaving a generous space in the centre of the room that he could use as he wished. However, as the opportunity was never used I stopped dismantling the guest king-size in this way as it was quite a strenuous exercise for which he never seemed to be around at the right time to help!

Perhaps the collecting enthusiasm I found most puzzling was of a certain pattern of china. It began in a charity shop on one of our days out in nearby towns or holiday venues, when Gerry held up a little dish to show me as I looked at clothes. "This is pretty!"

he said. I agreed, and he bought it and brought it home. It was incredible how often we saw other objects with the same pattern of pink roses, deep blue forget-me-nots and old gold petals. Different items turned out to be by various manufacturers and his research revealed that the pattern was called Old Chintz. After a while I suggested that he had better put up a special shelf in the bedroom to accommodate the little vases etc. That was after he found, in one bric-a-brac shop in Scotland, three pairs of different-shaped vases and a little trinket dish. I could just about cope with pieces coming in one at a time, but this influx of multiple additions posed a challenge as to where to put them! I believe at the final count, in the last couple of years we were together, there were about 45. The hoard included teapots, a golden wedding cup and saucer, a cat about 10 inches high, soap trays, jugs, to name but a few. I must confess I was personally responsible for buying the largest pieces in that pattern for him. I wanted to say a special 'Thank you' for the lovely Victorian cupboards we'd been able to install in our kitchen after he received an inheritance from his mother, so when I saw a Victorian-style wash bowl and jug, I felt sure it would give him great joy. He said it would, so I bought it there and then. That was the day when he actually started, occasionally, to leave behind pieces he saw in that pattern if he was able to resist. What he resisted in that same shop was a full-size bucket and, of all things, a kettle as big as the copper ones you often see in antique shops. I was mightily relieved about that! At the height of finding this pattern of china almost everywhere we went, it seemed as if Gerry had a magnet drawing him to it.

It doesn't seem fair to class the book-gathering as part of a sort of mania for collecting. After all, so many people have vast numbers of books, many of which are never read. Since I've recently had to move to a much, much smaller house I was surprised to find that I possessed not a few myself. Now I have a policy of reading my non-fiction books in bed in the mornings so that, one by one, I can pass them on to charity bookshops when finished. Oh, and I'd like to be up-front about the fact that I've got my collection of thirty-two DVDs arranged in alphabetical order, though not my books. I've already told you we're apparently all somewhere on the spectrum, haven't I?!

Charles Lamb (1775-1834) evidently wrote a book called *The Two Races of Men* in which he refers to 'borrowers of books – those mutilators of collections, spoilers of the symmetry of shelves, and creators of odd volumes.'

I shall never dare to borrow another book, and I hope I wasn't a mutilator of Gerry's precious collections, though I admit that they did sometimes try my patience!

Chapter 6

HOW DO YOU THINK THAT MADE ME FEEL? – AND MORE 'FAUX PAS'!

We'd only been together a few weeks, if that, and I can't remember how on earth this comment came to be made as I've completely forgotten the context. However, as long as I live I shall remember what Gerry said then. Amidst all the superlatives and adoring comments he was making on a daily basis, he declared: "If you die before me, I shall get married again as soon as possible!" I was flabbergasted, and for a moment or two quite speechless. Then I said, with my wry sense of humour trying to help me cope with the hurt I felt: "Well, I hope you'll wait till after the funeral!" I was a bit quiet afterwards, so Gerry asked if anything had upset me. When I explained that I was a bit hurt, to think he could contemplate replacing me with such haste, he couldn't understand that at all and simply said he would hope I would do the same if he died before me (though as I'm almost five years older he expected it to be the other way round).

Looking at the chapter heading: *'How do you think that made me feel?'* we need to consider that this is something an Aspie just cannot do. Towards the end of our married life together there were two deeply, deeply hurtful things that Gerry wrote down concerning me. He was so baffled as to why I found them upsetting that I did my best to explain patiently, ending with: "So do you understand now why that hurt my feelings?" When he said he didn't, I knew by this time that he wasn't being stubborn, still less uncaring, despite the stage our relationship had reached. He was merely being totally honest. By this time I was beginning to get something of an understanding of Asperger Syndrome; so though I was saddened by Gerry's inability to 'put himself in my shoes', I wasn't exasperated by it. If I could have my time over again I would never have breathed a word to Gerry about my suspicions of his having mild AS. I was talking at times to a professional who was not only experienced in working with clients facing these kinds of challenge, but was also married to a partner who had been expertly diagnosed as having AS, even though it wasn't abundantly clear to either the partner or the expert until the testing process was well advanced.

This particular person (who has AS) had found it a relief to have the diagnosis, as it explained all kinds of struggles experienced over the years. It was in a moment of Gerry's extreme anguish about what he felt was a complete inability to 'dive into (his) emotions' – an essential process for a spiritual programme he was devoted to at the time – that I chanced to remark: "I think I may have part of the explanation for that." When he asked what that was, I said that I thought he might have mild AS. All I hoped to do by saying that was to save him from yet another episode of "I can never get anything right, I'm a failure", an attitude that seemed to have been deeply ingrained in him throughout most of his life, from all that he had told me over the years. In saying what I did, I wanted to assure him that his seeming inability to do this exercise that he'd repeatedly tried and felt he'd failed in was not his 'fault'. This remark of mine unfortunately had an effect a bit like releasing a railway truck from the shed that had contained it, sending it on an unstoppable journey down a gentle but steady decline. Though I tried to clarify that AS was in no way a mental or any other kind of illness, that it often affected highly intelligent and talented individuals, as he is, and was merely a different kind of brain-patterning, Gerry's first response was to ring the surgery to ask for a GP appointment to find out if he 'had it'. (When he'd done an on-line test for himself the results had put him well over onto the AS side of the scale rather than the neuro-typical side.)

I gather his appointment, with a GP he'd never seen before, was very brief; and the main question was: "Has it ever affected your work?" Gerry replied that it hadn't, so the GP said he didn't think it possible that he had it! This was a very limited exploration of the facts, and I could give a long chapter and verse of work situations that have been spoiled or curtailed by a lack of 'know-how' in diplomacy, and what is and isn't expedient to say. Gerry has always had very few friends, but one of his closest who was also a health professional with a good deal of experience of how the autistic spectrum manifests in children, was another person who assured him he didn't have it, though has since had a change of mind. Gerry certainly wanted to know more about it, which I thought could be a helpful sign and would enlighten us both. Tony Attwood's excellent book (*Asperger's Syndrome. A Guide for Parents and Professionals, 1998*) had been recommended to me as essential reading, and when Gerry tracked it down to the library in our nearest city it was he who took the initiative, when we were there for another reason, and suggested we went to borrow it. Before returning home we went for tea and cake in the library café and, reading only the Preface, that was it! He would look no further into the book. Once he read: "*…the pattern included a lack of empathy, little ability to form friendships, one-sided conversations, intense absorption in a special interest…*" he said crossly: "Oh, I see; I've got *no empathy* haven't I?" For him those two words meant that he didn't care at all about other people, whereas – as I tried to explain to him – he often showed great concern about other people. What seemed more difficult for him was to enter into other people's probable feelings about things, and likely (adverse) responses to things he was apt to say and do; for example asking a lady loudly, in public, how old she is, or how much someone earns, or paid for their house. (Of course Zoopla can give him the latter bit of information now!) He did always add: "If you don't mind me asking" – but by then he'd done so!

When we first got together Gerry voluntarily told me that he really wanted to give up his tobacco addiction, and asked if I would help him. I said I'd be glad to, and asked him to let me know when he was ready to start the process. I'm blessed with very strong will-power (which my late father often said he envied); but I know that when it comes to substance addiction, it's not an easy thing to give up. I did my best to be supportive of numerous repeated attempts on Gerry's part, but I think I didn't do very well. I hadn't bargained for the furtiveness and outright lying that true addiction can lead to. In my own value system (and we should each be allowed to have our own, I now believe) total honesty in response to straight questions is paramount; so

I didn't handle well the times when I'd ask Gerry how he was doing with cutting down, initially, and I'd later find out that what he'd told me was far from the truth. What affected me most of all was a huge fear that this man I adored with my whole being might ultimately die of tobacco-caused cancer, as my father had done. Whenever Gerry came off tobacco, or went back on it, he was like a totally different (and pretty horrible) person for a few days. This was so different from his usual way of being that I soon became adept at tracking when he was and wasn't on his tobacco, regardless of what he told me. One day, when for the umpteenth time he'd 'given up on giving up', I was utterly overcome with this fear and sadness that one day I could lose him at too young an age because of it, so I went upstairs where I hoped I'd be out of earshot and sobbed and sobbed my heart out, face down on the bed.

I realised that I was personally responsible for my reaction to all this. (Others would have perhaps reacted differently). So I decided to seek help from a Psychosynthesis Counsellor. I think this system of psychotherapy is wonderful, as years previously I had been to quite a few weekend workshops based on it, and a five-day residential to learn more. I really appreciate the way it embraces every aspect of human beings: body, mind, feelings, spiritual nature. Understanding how we all have several sub-personalities through life, which help us to adapt or even survive, is fascinating. I think my inner 'School Prefect' was around when I was supposed, and wanting, to be helping Gerry with his addiction! Not all the sub-personalities that we have needed earlier still serve us well now, and may need to be 'written out of our current script'. After I had had a very worthwhile first session with the counsellor she enquired whether Gerry might be willing to come along with me for the next few sessions, as she felt he'd 'been there' in all but bodily presence in that first session. He readily agreed, and some useful insights were gained by both of us. The counsellor said she could see how there was a huge amount of love and goodwill between us, which confirmed our own impression. In one of the sessions Gerry mentioned the time I was sobbing on the bed. He referred to it as my having a 'temper tantrum'. I was a bit shocked, to say the least, as in my book a temper tantrum involves shouting and screaming at the person you're angry with, and you certainly wouldn't go away in private without letting the other person know what had annoyed you. On that occasion what I was actually feeling was scared, disappointed, despairing and sad – oh, and also useless as a support, which is what he'd asked me to be in his expressed wish to give up tobacco once and for all. Whenever I noticed that Gerry obviously wasn't his usual cheery self and asked how *he* was feeling, the only way he could describe it was: "I'm not feeling that good." There seemed no other words available to him if it involved emotions. Incidentally, he did give up tobacco for a very long time, seemingly as a result of a cancer scare several years down the line; but I'm sad to say he returned to it after leaving me.

Any attempt of his to predict how I might feel about something very personal he said or did to me was, of course, effectively like trying to speak in a country where he didn't know a word of the native language. Thus it was that his responses to some of my distresses during our life together were, to say the least, somewhat unfeeling. A minor instance was after I'd fallen downstairs only six weeks before the eagerly-awaited wedding of my son and his fiancée, which was to be held, to our delight, in the magical village where Gerry and I had had our honeymoon, and all our subsequent wedding anniversary weekends. I cracked two or three ribs, with the result that I could only turn over in bed with excruciating pain and vocalising a suitable sound to express that. Gerry thought it great sport to laugh and imitate the noise I tried so hard to suppress.

On the theme of weddings, we travelled up to Gretna Green, at their invitation, for the wedding of my foster-daughter and her fiancé. We had declined the offer to join their extended family the day before in rented accommodation part way to the venue as I knew it would be a rumbustious gathering, not something that would appeal to me at all, and not something Gerry would have been able to even tolerate. We made our own way, setting off early on the Friday morning of the event and made it to Gretna in good time, only to find that there were three wedding venues in the town. With a bit of ingenuity we even made it to the correct one before the appointed hour, but as we checked our facts at the reception desk I became immediately concerned when I saw the look on the young man's face and saw an older female colleague get up from her desk in a nearby office to come and break some bad news to us. "I'm afraid the ceremony's been delayed until tomorrow", she said. "They had a bit of a problem where they were staying last night." We were none the wiser as, with a last-minute change of mind over my accessories, I'd left my mobile phone back home (where Jess had tried to get a message to me) and Gerry hadn't got Jess's number stored on his phone. Gerry insisted that we'd stay overnight where we'd planned, but that he was most definitely returning home after breakfast at the Guest House the next day, without going back to Gretna. He reasoned that we couldn't be sure it would all happen on the Saturday, as now planned, either. Although he assured me I could stay if I wished, you may imagine my reluctance to be there without him; and naturally we only had the one car with us. I'm a strong enough person to have done all that on my own, but not when it was unforeseen and I had no idea what all the circumstances were and how much support and companionship I might need. So I meekly returned home with him. What had happened was that there was a bit of a scuffle at a nightclub, which had caused the bridegroom and best man to be detained in police cells overnight! The wedding did indeed happen on the Saturday.

It must be more difficult for any person who has never brought up children of his or her own to have a full understanding of how important and deep that parent-child bond can go; and how much more so if the non-parent is on the autistic spectrum. During my years with Gerry it so happened that both my son and my daughter developed cancer in their early thirties. When I realised that my daughter's prognosis was not all that good Gerry did his best to cheer me up, saying: "Well, if she doesn't make it, that'll be alright. It'll just be that her time has come. We all go at the time that's right for us." I kind of know what he means, but, strange to say, I didn't find that any comfort at all in my time of enormous distress! I'd rather have had a very, very long hug and an optimistic remark like: "I'm sure she'll make it through" – which I'm happy to say she did, very courageously and triumphantly, ten years ago as I write.

By the way, in case you haven't noticed, I don't pretend to be a saint, so I won't say I *never* got annoyed with Gerry. Interestingly, if he could tell I was annoyed, he always immediately assumed he'd done something I didn't like, whereas it was just as likely to be that the washing machine had gone wrong, or someone hadn't turned up for an appointment, or the computer was playing up. If I did express any annoyance at something Gerry had done (always spoken at low volume!) he would immediately walk out of the room. However gentle I was, he later told me that anyone expressing displeasure at something he'd done always felt like a physical blow in his solar plexus.

Referring just now to equipment going wrong reminds me of the time I had a flat tyre half an hour or so before we had guests coming round for a meal. I had to make sure that, when he came in from teaching two pupils at their house, I didn't mention it, or he would have gone up to remove and change the wheel regardless of our needing to greet the friends when they arrived. For some things he was an impetuous man of action, without a second's delay. There was another time when we had agreed that the lounge carpet needed its biennial shampooing, so we booked to hire the Rug Doctor for a few hours, which he kindly went to fetch from the store. This was a task we always did together, and found it rather fun. Within an hour and a half it was usually all done, as a team effort. I obviously can't move furniture on my own, especially considering the minor spinal injury; and even the repeated emptying of the bucketsful of dirty water that the cleaning process produces is quite strenuous, and was usually performed by Gerry. On this occasion, however he went to check his emails for the second time in the first couple of hours of the morning and found there was a fault on his computer. I didn't see him again, despite my request for help, until it was the time that the carpet shampooer was due back in the store. Yes, a ten-day episode of back spasms followed for me!

Another way in which there was a seeming lack of consideration for me was when Gerry had people over to our house for studio learning or recording. I provided the snacks and meals in between the morning and afternoon sessions and, in the early years, weekend Bed and Breakfast too. Their talk about the morning's work continued as they came downstairs for lunch, bringing mugs from their 'elevenses' into the kitchen; and not a word was said to me, even when they got to the end of their sentence or topic – well, Gerry's sentences mostly! I guess if it had been a hotel they were in, ignoring the serving staff might seem acceptable to some. However, I was never on Gerry's 'staff' – well, not officially anyway! – so I felt I deserved to be included in the conversation as we sat down to a meal together, and would await a suitable juncture to join in. I was not willing to remain 'the invisible woman' in our own home. Similarly, I realised that if I was out among people whom Gerry knew, after our first few months together I would be likely to need to introduce myself as he rarely thought of doing so once the novelty of having me in his life had worn off!

All the best books on life-sharing relationships emphasise that it's good to share thoughts and feelings honestly. Now that I know a lot more about Asperger Syndrome I feel that this needs some qualification; though I'm not sure how I could have avoided the drastic effects of the incident I am about to relate. The first introduction to the 'spiritual' programme that eventually drove a massive wedge between us came about because a woman who regularly had physiotherapy from me had given me the initial book about it. She needed to have treatments in her own home because of long-term illness. Gerry would often come over to that town with me to shop in a supermarket we didn't have where we lived, as we liked certain of their lines. He would then call for me at her home and I would leave her resting after her treatment when he rang the bell. On one occasion, when I went there alone, she gave me the book, saying: "I'm not saying you need this, but – as I've told you – I've found it really wonderful and it's changing my life. If you find it's not for you, you can always pass it on to one of your patients." I replied that, as Gerry had always been a restless 'spiritual seeker' (though I didn't use the word restless) he might find it interesting. Some years before that we'd often watch the *Oprah Winfrey Show* at lunchtimes and listen to the various people she had on for a while. Gerry would then always order every book the person of the moment had written and enthuse about them for a while until the next one captured his interest even more.

Gerry became so interested in this new book that he and my patient spoke on the phone a few times and it was agreed that, the next time I went to give her a treatment, he would come in afterwards, having done the usual shopping, and they'd be able to meet face to face. I suppose partly because I had detected Gerry's waning interest in me for a while, and partly from my intuition, I began to feel anxious about the potential in this meeting. On the journey over, my anxiety became strong and palpable, so I decided to explain to Gerry how I was feeling and why. At the very least I knew he would see I wasn't my usual self at all while the three of us would be together. I knew it would take all my acting skills to ensure that I behaved as naturally as possible, so as not to compromise my professional relationship with my patient for the future. I just asked Gerry to please try to understand that, if I didn't seem myself in that meeting it was because I was feeling afraid that – since she and her partner had recently split up – he and she might feel drawn to getting close to each other, since this programme was so important to them and I didn't feel I could resonate with it myself. Gerry later alleged that I'd been 'trying to control his friendships', and this was one of the things that turned him away from me.

Chapter Seven

WHAT DO YOU EXPECT ME TO DO?

From time to time my mother (born in 1905) used to say: "Common sense is not that common." Little did she or I realise at the time that she was quoting Voltaire! Ralph Waldo Emerson also had something interesting to say about this valuable asset: "Common sense is genius dressed in its working clothes." But it may be that there's a type of genius that simply cannot, in this way, put on 'its working clothes'. My particular adorable Aspie often seemed at a loss as to how to proceed, and a friend of mine, who's married to one, says he stands in the kitchen and asks what needs doing when, to her – and me – it would be perfectly obvious. The expression "That goes without saying…" is not a helpful one where people with AS are concerned. Also it's as well to remember that words and expressions may be taken very literally.

I've explained that in those early days of living together many of my belongings needed to be shunted to far corners of the house so that Gerry could have a lot of his own things close at hand in the sitting room. One day I was clearing out some things I'd kept for ages and felt would have to go now. As a good number of these were large paintings and drawings done by my children when they were small, Gerry decided to light a bonfire at the far end of the garden. There was no recycling service then and Gerry loved lighting fires, so I let him get on with it. While he was busy with that I was re-arranging books in a bookcase, checking if any could now go to second-hand shops so that I could free up a couple of shelves for my things transferred from downstairs. The bigger books were easy to pile up on the floor, and for the very small ones, like old volumes of single-author poetry, it was convenient to pop them into an empty waste-paper basket while I made a different space for them all. I was absorbed in my task, and Gerry came and went a couple of times with old cardboard from the loft etc, and it was only when I turned round to a better crouched position that I saw that the waste-paper basket had vanished. I hurried up to the bonfire just in time to see a beautiful pink suede-bound volume of one of my favourite poets beginning to smoulder, as well as one or two other small books. I tried to rescue them and Gerry was mortified and devastated to think he had damaged something that was precious to me. I was much more concerned about his profound distress than the loss of the books (which were beyond hope by then), because he clearly hadn't intentionally destroyed them. It was merely a misinterpretation of something he saw: Books in a waste-paper basket, therefore waste paper! Given how important books have always been in his own life, and that one of mine was in a very special rare binding, it's extraordinary that he didn't at least check with me what my intentions were before whisking them away to be burned. But then, *he* is extraordinary in so many ways, and it's part of what I adore about him.

Although he definitely had a secretive side, especially in our later years together, if Gerry was talking openly his honesty was uninhibited; I almost wrote 'uncensored'. Two instances of this definitely affected his work progress. Prior to the one year of full-time teaching, he had held a part-time post at the same establishment, but naturally had to be re-interviewed. One of his colleagues gave very helpful feedback after this, commenting that, when asked about any weaknesses he had, Gerry had mentioned that he very often didn't keep to lesson plans if the students side-tracked onto something really interesting. Now, I don't think that necessarily makes him a less good teacher; in fact it may well be the reverse. Certainly, when the one-year contract was not extended, many of his students were up in arms, protesting that he was their best teacher and that when *he* explained things they could really understand them. What the colleague advised was: "Well, you wouldn't say that in an interview!" With his lack of interest in 'worldly wisdom' Gerry would have no doubt been thinking, if not saying, his classic retort: "Well, I just did!"

This same colleague kindly invited the two of us, together with another new recruit and his wife, for a meal in his home. After the main course he and his wife needed to put their two children to bed, so brought an apple crumble and a one-litre tub of ice cream to the table, telling us to help ourselves, and they'd be back with us shortly. Unfortunately Gerry got hold of the ice cream first, and didn't think to mentally divide it into six before serving his own portion. I noticed with horror that he nonchalantly took about a third of it, without a second thought. (Yes, I realise that many other people might well have done this if they were as fond of ice cream and large portions as he is!)

The other work-related faux-pas that I got to know about had much more serious repercussions. Every summer a huge part of Gerry's income came from assessing work in one of his specialisms for an exam board. There were a couple of days of residential training for this each year, a few weeks before the exams were taken. He was highly-thought-of with this work, and tricky cases were often referred on to him by supervisors if other examiners had doubts. They also valued the fact that he would take on extra batches of marking if any colleagues fell by the wayside for health or other reasons. So by the time of the particular training session that 'got him into hot water' he was very experienced and confident. Over one of the meal-times on the initial training day a first-timer he was sitting next to asked how on earth it was possible to listen to such a large volume of long recordings, then assess and mark them in the allotted time. Gerry, repeating what a different chief examiner had recommended a few years earlier, said that the knack was to listen to the whole thing for the first so many students, till you got the hang of it, then for later ones just sample a fair bit from the beginning and the end, omitting some minutes in the middle. The following morning, on the telephone, I heard the unmistakable voice of a very crestfallen Gerry saying that he was coming home straight away. Someone overheard the previous day's conversation, reported him to the chief examiner and he was summarily dismissed; so bang went the vast majority of his summer earnings.

I'm aware that this book is something of a miscellany of recollections, as things spring to mind. Some, as you will have noticed, are fairly trivial, whilst others have more serious implications. The basic theme in this chapter is broadly about the difficulty some people with Asperger's seem to have in grasping what is obvious to, or at least easier for, neuro-typical people. Some examples also cover a feeling of being at a loss as to how to respond in an unusual situation, or feeling overwhelmed by tasks that others might take to quite naturally. Reflecting on these may mean that, if a partner has awareness of the challenges that even everyday situations may present, hopes and expectations can be tempered accordingly; and hopefully extra supplies of compassion and patience can be found – though preferably offered in a non-patronising way. What an opportunity for personal development!

Another bit of damage that Gerry felt mortified about was the destruction of the heatproof glass lid of one of our set of saucepans. The smallest one of the set, really intended just for heating milk, didn't have a lid supplied with it, so on the rare occasions when it needed a lid I would borrow the one belonging to the next size up, and this would sit perfectly securely on top. Having seen me do this on several occasions, Gerry did the same when cooking a small amount of vegetables when the other pans were already in use, or one still in the washing-up. The difference between his way of using it and mine was that he was always apt to have the gas turned up to the highest possible flame, at least initially. Unfortunately it hadn't occurred to him that the glass was not manufactured for actual contact with flames, so there was a resounding cracking noise as it split in half. Fortunately the metal rim still held the lid together, but it couldn't be used any more.

We were both self-employed – well, Gerry mainly so; and with his performing music often involving evening and weekend work, we had an agreement to both give two hours to 'home care' on alternate Friday mornings. (Home care sounds much more appealing than housework, doesn't it?!) We would make a list of tasks that needed doing just occasionally and then see which each of us felt like doing that day, or find one or two that needed both pairs of hands. That day Gerry opted to lift the secondary-glazing panels out of the dining room sash window so as to clean the three glass surfaces reachable from the inside and clear out the cobwebs which sneaky spiders had woven between the two panes. The secondary panels were pretty heavy but he's strong, and turned down my offer of assistance to place them back in position. There were two sliding plastic wedges that kept the panel from moving from side to side once back in position. Suddenly there was a great thud as the lower panel slid down unchecked, hitting Gerry's thumb. I rushed over at once to administer help, first aid and comfort and he immediately burst into anguished tears welling up from way down low, saying: "I'm never going to live up to your expectations!" We were both deeply upset, and I didn't quite know what to make of this, as the whole enterprise had been undertaken voluntarily. My best guess is that it was an unfamiliar task, he felt he'd shown himself incapable and therefore felt utterly overwhelmed and wretched. My only concern was that he'd hurt himself, but if I remember correctly, on this occasion he needed to rush away and be by himself. Although this was, on the surface, a purely domestic task, it clearly touched distressing emotions in a deep place within Gerry.

One morning I woke up with a jolt at about 5 a.m. and realised that Gerry wasn't in bed beside me. Just a few times in our 17 years together he would have something on his mind and be wakeful in the middle of the night, in which case he'd go straight to the computer in his home office and surf the internet. On this occasion he was absolutely nowhere to be seen. I threw my dressing-gown over my nightdress and went up the road to where we parked our cars, only to find his gone. What on earth could have happened? The previous evening there'd been a bit of tension between us over something, but it all seemed resolved by bedtime and we'd chatted and cuddled each other as usual before going to sleep. I was beside myself, waiting for it to get light. I knew what time the people opposite where we parked usually took their dog for the first walk of the day, so I waylaid them and asked if by chance they'd been aware of Gerry driving off in the early hours, and if so, at what time. I know this wouldn't have solved the mystery of where he'd gone, but any kind of information was better than none. Gerry did carry a mobile phone, but never left it switched on. It was merely for convenience, in case of breakdown, or to let me know what time to expect him after he'd set off home from a gig I hadn't attended. The neighbours couldn't tell me anything, so I just decided to make a cup of tea and sit and wait and work out what to do and when.

I think it was about 9 a.m. when he returned home, totally surprised I'd been anxious, and explained that he'd woken up in the night with a searing pain in his eye, so had taken himself off to the Accident and Emergency department of a hospital ten miles away to get it checked over. When I asked why on earth he hadn't woken me so that I could have come with him he said: "Well I know you always say you need your sleep, so I thought

I'd better not disturb you." I explained that I would always wish him to wake me if he was in any kind of distress, even if I had to do a full day's work at my distant Clinic the next day, though on that day I wasn't in fact due to go there. He hadn't thought to write a note, or to ring me from the hospital at any point. Both of those things might have been a bit difficult to do under the circumstances; but the point is that it at no time entered his head that his sudden unexplained absence might worry me!

A while later a real crisis occurred where, if common sense had been available, it could have saved a very sad situation. Although the thorough check-up at A & E hadn't led to any particular advice (though I think some soothing drops may have been prescribed) the incident just described may have been a forewarning of what was to follow some weeks or months later. Gerry's eye hadn't been totally comfortable for a while, he later told me, so he was glad a regular optician's appointment was coming up. He always arranged these on a day when he was teaching in that town anyway, to avoid a 44-mile round trip just for that. I happened to be looking after my grandson in Leicestershire and was to be away overnight as usual. I wasn't able to speak to him on my safe arrival as I normally did because I knew he had the appointment, but I left a message to that effect on his home office answer-phone. It appears that, when the optician made the eye examination, she said that it looked as if his retina was detaching and that he should go straight to the hospital there. He asked if he'd be able to drive home if they put drops in his eye and, on hearing that he wouldn't be safe to do so for a while afterwards, decided that he wouldn't report to any hospital that day.

I do wish she'd impressed upon him that a detached retina can have very serious consequences, as he didn't seem to have ever known that. He didn't phone me at my son's house to report this, and we never had the opportunity to phone each other on the Tuesday evenings I was away because of his late return home from his choir rehearsal. So the first I knew about any of this was the evening of the day I got back, when he mentioned it casually. In fact I rather think it was even a day after that, as he'd been out doing another conducting job. I insisted that he ask for an emergency appointment with our GP and discovered that he'd given the optician the wrong name of the surgery we were registered at, so none of the referral information had gone through. Suffice it to say that I drove Gerry for an early appointment locally, then a twenty-two mile dash to the hospital he'd been near two days earlier, where a young lady doctor gave him a bit of a ticking off for his casual attitude. She managed to book him in for an emergency operation at a specialist city hospital sixty miles away, via a route we didn't know, that was likely to take an hour-and-a-half under good conditions. Fortunately she printed a map for us, but it was essential that we got there by 12 noon, or we'd miss the slot. Despite road works and diversions we made it there with five minutes to spare, and then began the long round of repeated history-taking by different members of staff, with the operation being done by an eminent surgeon at about 6 p.m. I was able to wait till Gerry came back to the ward, then drove my weary way back home to sleep like the dead until he woke me about 7 a.m. next morning to say that I could go and collect him right away, he was just waiting for his drops to be dispensed and could see better than he had since age eight. I'm sorry to say that that was a temporary state of improvement.

If he wasn't entirely sure how to look after himself properly, it must have been even more puzzling to know how to set about looking after anyone else. On the two or three occasions when I was unwell and needed his care, he would bring me my usual breakfast, ask if I wanted lunch at some time or other when he surfaced from the computer! – and that's all I'd see of him all day and evening. This is not a criticism: if he was unwell he liked to just sleep and sleep and sleep and not be disturbed, so since my needs are different from his, it's only reasonable that I would need to make my request known. Once, after we'd done a supermarket shop in a nearby town where we went every six weeks or so, I fell over in the car park as we were walking back to the car. Within seconds I was surrounded by three or four other shoppers asking what they could do to help, while one had gone to call the store's first-aider. From the moment I fell, Gerry just stood looking down at me, with a completely baffled expression on his face, as if wondering: "What should I do now?" He didn't even speak to me to ask if I was alright. Luckily I wasn't badly hurt, and it was also fortunate that – by this time – I was getting well-used to reactions from Gerry that seemed very different from those of most other people that I knew. I just didn't have any explanation for them at that stage.

Chapter Eight

I'M ALL YOURS

With hindsight – especially after I'd been left on my own – I began to realise that Gerry had a very unusual way of forming attachments to people. I suppose I found it mildly amusing (and perhaps a little shocking!) to learn from him that, while at Music College, he'd had thirty different 'partners'; though I think many were 'one night stands'. It was not that he wanted them to be; but he said that most of them hadn't wanted to see him again afterwards. I had various thoughts on this lively love life. One was: "Whatever would my mother think if she were still alive and got to know that I'd accepted a proposal from, and indeed married, a Lothario, Casanova (or whatever title might be suitable)?" Mother's was a fairly strait-laced viewpoint and apparently, according to her youngest sister, she hadn't enjoyed the physically intimate side of marriage at all. I was always glad that I hadn't inherited this attitude, though as a student I did 'save myself' for marriage. Gerry's student days were in the even more permissive 70s; so I'm sure thirty partners in three years may not have been exceptional.

He was about twenty-two when he married his first wife Barbara, and she was not the woman with whom he'd fathered a child at nineteen. I once asked him what had inspired him to marry Barbara. He replied: "She seemed to think I was OK. No-one else did." They married in a register office, fairly swiftly I believe, and I'm pretty sure it was before his family had even met her. By the time she was introduced it was a fait accompli. A Blessing Ceremony in his home church enabled family members to celebrate the marriage. Since his four-year affair with a work colleague began after only about six years with his first wife, I imagine Barbara didn't fulfil all his hopes and expectations, or meet the criterion I shall refer to with great significance later. I can't recall hearing whether he ever asked his lover if she would marry him. She herself was in an 'open marriage' and had a young daughter.

The next significant attachment he formed was with a woman he met in an band they were both playing in. I seem to remember his saying that this falling in love also struck him like lightning. He had moved in with her and her children pretty quickly. His view was that she had been glad of his arrival to get her out of an unsatisfactory marriage, but that when she discovered he couldn't hand her £100 every Monday morning to go and buy clothes at the nearest shopping mall, as her husband had done, she soon asked him to move out. He also felt that the eldest child had tried to engineer his removal, which happened after a few months. He said little about what his wife thought of how their marriage ended; but I do know his lover had been furious at the arrival of a new woman in his life as she evidently declared to Gerry: "This relationship isn't over until I say it is!" Dear Reader, keep this slighted ex-lover in mind, as she re-appears later in the story!

Gerry asserted to me that he was perfectly content living in a bed-sit on his own after this sorry sequence of events. Nevertheless it was not very long before his next romance began. His version of events is that, after playing in a folk club organised by a couple in Manchester, the woman had soon afterwards attended another gig where he was playing, this time without her partner. She made overtures to him and moved out to a flat when their relationship started, but when they got together completely they managed to persuade her previous partner to move out of the large house they'd shared so that she and Gerry could occupy it, with tenants for extra income. Altogether he and Juliet (same name as the partner with children that he lived with briefly, and my name also!) were together for ten years. After about five years they moved to Derbyshire, near the town where I had my main clinic and, curiously, I got to know her before I knew him well as she came to me for physiotherapy quite a number of times. When he brought her along for her appointments I observed how attentive and adoring he seemed to be towards her. I was a little envious, my first marriage having ended by then.

Having seen this seemingly adoring and devoted manner, little did I guess that Gerry was to have two affairs with different women during the course of living with Juliet II. The first of those was on-and-off over a period of a couple of years, and the second lasted just a few months, until the partner he lived with asked him to move out definitely for good; and who could blame her? – since the wronged husband concerned had notified her of Gerry's first affair at the time he'd discovered it. He'd been made to move his belongings out to a bed-sit at that point, but I'm not sure he'd even spent a night there before he wheedled his way back.

According to what he told me, he'd declared his willingness to go for relationship counselling sessions, but Juliet hadn't wished to do that.

We're now approaching the point where I come into Gerry's chequered love life! The day after his birthday, Juliet said she wanted him to leave after about six weeks at the latest. Much later he told me he could never understand why she wanted to go along with him while he was flat-hunting. I explained that I would have felt the same, namely, 'as this is a man I have loved for years and years, I should like to see where he will be living from now on, even though I have asked him to leave' (not that I'd ever been in that position). As this was all happening while he was still very fond of Fran, the other woman he'd had the most recent affair with, he asked her if he was to look for a flat for one, or the two of them. She replied that, though she was very fond of Gerry, there was another man whom she'd really loved for years, and that they'd recently met up again and hoped to make a future together. With something like an 'Oh well…!' Gerry rushed off to Manchester to see the ex-colleague he'd had the four-year affair with; but – as he put it to me soon afterwards – "After twenty-four hours with her I realised I couldn't be what she wanted me to be." I never got further detail on what that was exactly. However, nothing daunted, he remembered how a mutual friend of his and mine, knowing he was being asked by his partner to leave, had told him she thought that he and I would get on really well and that her expert knowledge of serious astrological analysis showed this too.

What followed is the sequence of events in my opening

chapter; that is, our 'whirlwind romance'! Anyone reading the current chapter and realising that most of this was declared to me in our first days together – the disarming honesty I referred to – may well wonder why I ever agreed to be his wife. I guess I'm an optimist and, as I said, convinced that Gerry had never found the right one to understand him before, and that I was the one who could be that person. How is it the old song goes?

> *I'd sacrifice everything, come what might*
> *For the sake of having you near,*
> *In spite of a warning voice that comes in the night*
> *And repeats and repeats in my ear:*
> *"Don't you know, little fool,*
> *You never can win.*
> *Use your mentality;*
> *Wake up to reality.*
> *But each time I do just the thought of you*
> *Makes me stop before I begin,*
> *'Cos I've got you under my skin.*

That's exactly how it was: Gerry got under my skin and is still there, I'm pretty certain, for good.

A friend of mine who qualified and practised as a Clinical Psychologist was very interested when, a while after Gerry left, I mentioned that I was reflecting on his unusually rapid way of forming passionate attachments to a series of women. It seemed so extreme that I was wondering if it was some kind of attachment disorder. From my very basic study of Child Development as a trainer of Playgroup leaders in the mid 1970s, I had read John Bowlby's work on the importance of attachment, but didn't know anything much about disorders of this nature. The Psychologist told me that Asperger Syndrome and Attachment Disorders quite often co-exist. Having seen him 'go through' a number of relationships, a member of his family remarked to me: "Whenever Gerry goes into a relationship and it ends, he leaves disaster in his wake."

In Gerry's case he had told me a great deal about how he never felt a sense of belonging in his family, to the extent that he used to fantasise that perhaps he'd landed in the wrong one. Physical resemblances make it pretty certain that there was no mix-up at the hospital; but this is how strongly alienated he felt. As to the death of his father when Gerry was seven, he told me that his very first thought when he was told was: "Good; now I shan't be beaten any more." All credible reports I've heard describe his father as a lovely, warm-hearted and not overly strict man. One of his sons, born to a mother who died when he was young, vouched for the fact that Gerry may have been given a smack now and then (not uncommon in parenting in that era) but was certainly never 'beaten'. Gerry recalled how, in class on the day of his father's funeral he looked at the clock and thought, very matter-of-factly: "Oh, my Dad's being put in the ground now." When I first got together with him and was saying how awful it must have been to be so young when he lost his dad, even though he was a relatively elderly father, Gerry said with conviction: "Not really. It didn't affect me at all, but maybe it did my sister." She had gone on to have emotional and psychological problems later on in her life and has needed a lot of support at times. Fortunately, when she reached her late forties, she married a good man and they seem just right for each other.

Gerry's closest friend for the majority of the years of our life together was Fran, the last woman he had an affair with before he and I got together. I liked her immensely and, since she married not long after we did, each couple attended the other's wedding celebrations. I thought it was very considerate of her when Gerry told me she'd asked him if I minded their ongoing contact, mainly in musical contexts. One reason she enquired was that her new husband had told her he felt uneasy if she ever spent time with her ex-husband. I can't remember if Gerry asked me first, (I think not!) but he assured her I didn't have any problem with their friendship. It is true that during all the years when he made it very clear to me and everybody around that he adored and admired me (and this was mutual), I was perfectly relaxed about the time he spent with other women in the context of his work. Needless to say that, with a history like his, I kept an eye open for any signs that he was getting extremely interested in any particular one, and this was more marked as he began to show less and less interest and spend less and less time with me. The advent of the internet in our home certainly made a very big difference to our relationship, as I am sure it has done to many that were established in the days before that phenomenon spread pretty well everywhere. To my mind it's had a much worse effect on marriages and close relationships than the clichéd cameo of the man hidden behind the newspaper at the breakfast table every morning! In addition to all the things Gerry collected at home, by the time we'd been together about twelve years he had 'collected' conductorships of four choirs, some of these posts being unpaid; so we almost became like ships that passed in the night with all the demands of regular rehearsals.

The reason I've mentioned his best friend Fran at this point in the saga is that, when Gerry first left me and moved in with his current wife, she and her husband expressed genuine sympathy with me and my plight but explained that they 'couldn't take sides'. I fully understood that, didn't want them to and acknowledged that she had, after all, been Gerry's friend long before he knew me properly. She was the person he could confide in when things began to go badly wrong for our marriage, and I had prepared her and her husband by explaining all the context when the rift was about to happen, as I suspected that he would need lots of emotional support at that point – little knowing that my successor was just coming into view. He still did need her support anyway, so I was not wrong there. In the context of his professional life Fran and her husband have had to have a great deal of contact with Gerry and his third wife, so I kept as discreetly in the background for this couple as I could, whilst still keeping in touch with Fran through serious illnesses she and her husband had. She and I have recently become good friends in our own right, and that's how I know what Gerry replied when she asked him, near the end of our life together, if he had really loved me. The word she used to me was that he'd said yes, he was really smitten; so she'd then asked him if the marriage couldn't be saved – she thought it could. He replied that 'things had gone too far'.

Intimate relationships are not the only ones that Gerry seems to find it difficult to sustain. Throughout the years I knew him well he never had any friend that he would hang out or meet up with, other than the men who shared his hobby, and that would only be at AGMs or exhibitions. On the whole they would be in touch exclusively about hobby events, though there were a couple of guys he would, from time to time, have long phone calls with, one of whom was in the music world. It's interesting that the 'falling in love' episode with the woman who lived abroad, for whom he broke off his first engagement to me, also happened over the telephone. When he was faced with the reality of being with the woman, he couldn't stand her!

In concluding this chapter it seems appropriate to mention the phenomenon of '**splitting**'[1] which has affected not only me, but also more recently his close friend Fran. This is something entirely different from splitting up; it's a term to describe the diametrically opposed view taken of someone who has 'fallen from grace' in the eyes of the initiator of this attitude, compared with the idealisation, and perhaps adoration that was felt before. I gather it most often occurs in people with 'Borderline Personality' Profile. In chapter one I described how Gerry 'worshipped' me and put me on a pedestal, and I remarked that, if you are put up on a pedestal, there is only one way to go. In my case the topple was horrendous. In the new couple's haste to get married after Gerry left me, a divorce petition against me was drawn up

---

[1] **Splitting** (*verywell.com* definition): "a very common defence mechanism leading sufferers to view others, themselves and life events in all or nothing terms" and on the *After Psychotherapy* website: "One minute they may love and revere you, the next turn on you with vicious anger… To some extent splitting and its companion defense, projection, plays a role in most psychological disorders."

which bore little or no resemblance to how my life with Gerry had been. I could only show it to two of my three closest and most trusted friends and they were people who'd spent a great deal of time with us through the years of our marriage. They were aghast and incredulous. When I showed the Mediator (who was trying to help us to reach a fair financial settlement) a typed list of beautiful, admiring and appreciative remarks Gerry had made to me, most of which were dated – on the advice of a Counsellor I was seeing – he noticed how recently very many of these had been said. Gerry himself had told me that his new fiancée had "never come across a couple divorcing who weren't slagging each other off" and that he'd told her I was "an amazing woman". All that was before I tried to safeguard my rights in respect of the house, which had been mine for two-and-a-half years before he came into my life with £2,500 of debt, which I helped him to pay off.

And the marital 'crimes' I had committed that had made him stop loving me? Well the major ones were that, at sixty-five I said I intended to retire fully when I reached seventy-one, which was when the endowment policy would mature to pay off the mortgage; and that I didn't think it wise to try to buy a property bigger than our three-storey, four-bedroom Victorian semi-detached house which, in addition, had the flatlet where Gerry had his own work space. I wouldn't have thought it wise even if we had had the money, which we most definitely didn't. Once I'd seen what Gerry had written about wanting, among other things, a bigger house, more money and a 'perfect relationship' I naturally asked if he was on the look-out for somebody new, and he admitted that he was. Other women friends of mine have told me they weren't surprised that, thereafter, I kept an eye on who his emails on our shared email address were coming from and began to question him about a woman he often spent time with, the one who had passed on the book and thus introduced him to a 'spiritual programme' that promised people they could have 'the fulfilment of all (their) life's dreams.' By the way, Gerry's definition of a 'perfect relationship' was 'one that meets all my needs at all levels'.

Gerry was, understandably, really upset that, having read most of the first book in the spiritual programme he was following, I described the teaching as selfish. However, I was being honest about how it came across to me. As for 'lesser crimes', I think I've already mentioned that I didn't agree to the double guest room becoming solely a hobby room. Also 'the trouble (was)' that I don't play a musical instrument; that (oddly enough!) "your family are very nice and that, but they're no blood relations of mine"! There was also an allegation that I'd 'wanted to take over' Gerry's bank account. This arose from a consideration of our imminent need to get a new central heating boiler and have the outside of the house painted, concerns I'd pointed out in the context of why it seemed unwise to aspire to moving to somewhere even bigger. I'd prepared a document called a Finance Review to make these things clearer, suggesting a little of his money as well as mine might be put aside towards such things and perhaps something given to me towards my hair-dos etc now that I was semi-retired and he was doing well for work at that time and earning considerably more than me. But I had specifically typed: "Up to now Gerry and Juliet have maintained separate bank accounts, apart from equal monthly contributions to the 'holidays and occasional meals out' fund, which is joint, and it would seem wise to continue this arrangement". As you can see, this was another misinterpretation of what I was actually stating, even though it was in black and white this time, rather than just spoken.

I guess another shortcoming I had was that I'm not mad about watching science fiction all that often; and that when Gerry suddenly landed in my life I wasn't willing, crazy about him though I was, to let him choose the TV viewing exclusively, especially since in the early months together, with his having only an hour or two of work each week and no internet, he was viewing in our only downstairs reception room all day and all evening. What I negotiated, and he agreed to, was alternate days for each of us to choose when and what to view, and the theory was to plan and choose weekend viewing in consultation with each other and the *Radio Times*. Somehow, that never quite happened. With hindsight, I suspect this lack of being able to have his own way over TV all the time was one thing that made him very unhappy. I'd never in my life come across anyone who watched TV for so many hours on end. My guess now is that it's one way to shut other people out and keep control over conversational intimacy; and also, in Gerry's case, to block out unwanted thoughts, especially in those early months when he'd shot straight from one life-sharing relationship into another (and has now done the same again.) More about Gerry's taste in TV will be revealed in the chapter of miscellaneous bits which follows.

Chapter Nine

POINTS OF VIEWING

One interesting thing to observe is how an Aspie gets on with other people manifesting signs of the syndrome. In the course of his teaching, Gerry would come home and mention new pupils who'd been assigned to him for instrumental lessons at the start of a new academic year or term. Among these from time to time were several with Asperger Syndrome – otherwise I'm not sure he would ever have heard of it. I gathered he found it a bit of a struggle to deal with some of them. I only got to meet one, as she came for lessons at the house. From what he told me I think it bugged Gerry that, following the mother's request, he had to break each one-hour lesson into two parts as Alice couldn't sustain concentration for the full time. In the mid-break Alice would babble on intensely about whatever was pre-occupying her at the time, and Gerry found this very difficult to tolerate. He hates interruptions anyway. I believe these lessons continued for a couple of years, but Gerry became more and more exasperated with them as time went on and I think was relieved when Alice decided to discontinue, despite the loss of income which was always a blow to him.

I think it was only as I was trying to recover from Gerry's abrupt departure, and I was relying much more on TV myself, for company, that I began to reflect on the programmes we'd both liked watching with apparently equal enjoyment. These are still a precious way for me to be reminded happily of old times. For him, Sci-Fi was top of the list; but as I said, I couldn't share that enthusiasm to anything like the same degree. Factual ones like *Grand Designs* and *Antiques Roadshow* were mutually acceptable. On the whole, Gerry merely tolerated the various detective series that I loved watching and then only sometimes, as he would often walk out of the room – especially once he'd got the internet in his home office. However he did absolutely love watching *New Tricks*, as do I. I can't exactly remember when we started following that because we were rather later than most people in getting a digital box, so were restricted to five channels only until about four years before he left. (We were both quite proud, in a way, of having oldish cars, a very old quality TV my brother had cast off prior to 1989 with superb sound and colour, old hand-me-down mobile phones and second-hand computers. We couldn't ever afford new versions of any of those things, except perhaps the phones, had we wanted to.) So I suspect I knew little or nothing about Asperger's in adults when I first became acquainted with Brian Lane, perhaps the most arrestingly unusual – no pun intended – of the original bunch of retired policemen working for UCOS (Unsolved Crime and Open cases Squad). They are all pretty markedly individual, including Jack Halford who misses his deceased wife so much that he sits and talks to her at the little shrine with candles and her ashes that he's made in his garden. I'm right with him there. When your beloved is suddenly snatched away you still have a lot to say, and things you wish you could still tell them about the day's events face to face.

Returning to the character Brian Lane, he has encyclopaedic knowledge about criminal cases in the past, recalling accurately all the dates, information and connections. If he doesn't have all the information at his fingertips – and he usually does – he seems to know ways that haven't occurred to his colleagues to ferret it out, and indeed doesn't rest until he has done. At times when he's not officially allowed to be working because of a recurrence of a drink problem, or failing to take medication that controls his moods, he will still compulsively get to work on the current case and is usually the one with a stroke of genius that unblocks an impasse in the investigations. He is always puzzled by reactions in others that his colleagues could have told him would be likely to ensue; and though he clearly adores his wife Esther in his own quaint fashion, he often has funny ways of showing it and sometimes drives her to the brink of despair. He just has such difficulty in demonstrating his affection for her in ways she can appreciate, and when she is confined to bed after an accident his colleagues have to show him how to care for someone. He sets up a walkie-talkie radio so she can let him know when she needs something, but needless to say that on one occasion when she calls him, he's too absorbed in the case he's working on to even notice that she's speaking to him. Another lovable Aspie, I suspect!

So much for the only detective series that Gerry did like watching. Where films were concerned we both loved some classic 'Romcoms' like *Sleepless in Seattle, Love Actually, You've got Mail*, and a good few more, which we watched many times.

Gerry's romantic side was very special and precious to me indeed, and I was so sad when it began to fade, which did not happen for at least fourteen years. As regards the TV series that focussed on personal relationships, communities etc. he loved *Last of the Summer Wine* and *Dad's Army* (I didn't, though I could tolerate them sometimes) but not much else like that apart from *Doc Martin* and *Frasier*. I remember my astonishment the first time he watched an episode of *Doc M*, clearly enjoyed it and became a 'regular'. If you've seen even one episode yourself, you'll know how incredibly tactless the Doc habitually was: rudely blunt in fact; and also how seemingly oblivious he was to the adverse effect this had on his patients and the Cornish village community in general. Whenever Louisa, who at first became the closest thing he had to a friend, tried to explain why things he'd said had upset and distressed people, he looked utterly baffled. Eventually the two of them got closer and eventually married – after a few hiccups – but he never had a clue about when he was being deeply hurtful in how he acted towards her and some of the things he said, especially when she was pregnant and then in labour. As a doctor he undoubtedly knows his stuff very well, and for this the village community takes him to their heart in many ways and he often becomes the hero of the hour. But along with the expert knowledge he has there is no knowledge – or precious little – of human nature, to guide him as to when a long technical speech about detailed medical diagnoses or prognoses is appropriate, and when not. With Martin Clunes' brilliant acting many viewers must surely ache for his character as they see him yearning to be really loved and probably also longing to learn how to love appropriately if he wants a long-term life-sharing partnership. Like Doc Martin, Gerry didn't suffer fools gladly; and I'm sorry to say he put more than a few people in that category.

Gerry also watched *About a Boy* with special interest, and some distress, I seem to recall; but most of all *ET*, which never failed to bring him, and usually me, to tears at the end. I realise with hindsight how much he could probably identify with feeling like an alien in an often-baffling world. If you'll forgive the pun, it's sad that Gerry so often Alien-ates so many people who start out being very fond of him. Of course, in Gerry's favourite Sci-Fi series, the character Data, being a robot, has to have all emotions explained to him, as far as possible, in rational terms of speech. Gerry was nowhere near that state of unknowing. Nevertheless, as our relationship declined – and at the start of that neither of us wanted it to happen – he proved true to what Tony Attwood's excellent book refers to as the difficulty of 'emotional repair.' [When Gerry at last agreed, about eighteen months before we parted, that we could go together to share about our increasing estrangement with a mutually-trusted friend whom he chose – formerly a spiritual teacher he'd respected greatly – she prepared a simple mirror-image questionnaire for each of us. The simple questions were: "What are you seeking from / able to give to your partner", and then the same two questions applied to the marriage. As I pondered and started to write down my replies Gerry, after about five minutes, said: "I can't answer any of this".]

The oddest thing that happened over our viewing on 'the box' (this time a video rather than TV) was when Gerry bought

Groundhog Day in a charity shop. We really enjoyed watching it together, and I hadn't seen the film before, whereas I think he must have watched it on TV at least once or twice. Often at weekends, especially Saturday nights, there were no scheduled programmes that captured the interest of either of us; so I nearly always invited Gerry to choose which video or DVD we would watch. That way I could be fairly sure of my favourite kind of evening, snuggled up together on the sofa, as we had done most evenings during the first five or six years together until his evening work got busier (and until we had the cuddly cat!). We watched said film now and then, in amongst all the others we had to choose from until an extraordinary thing happened, and he suggested watching *Groundhog Day* every three or four days for a period of a few weeks. If you've watched it yourself you'll see how amusing that is, given that the whole theme of the film is of an identical day that keeps repeating itself until the 'spell' is broken. I don't think I made any comment about this seemingly endless repetition of viewing the same film as by this time I'd realised that Gerry had periods of puzzling behaviour that it was best to go along with until they worked themselves through. All films that had the theme of time travel (e.g. *Field of Dreams, Sliding Doors*) held a special fascination for him, and I enjoyed most of those too, especially *The Time Traveller's Wife.*

In the end Gerry took to a most bizarre way of watching TV or films, wearing headphones. This was great if it was a programme I didn't want to watch at all, (e.g. a film starring Arnold Schwarzenegger, Jackie Chan or war programmes). As a natural pacifist and rather a sensitive soul I truly find it horrendous to see images of fighting whether they be in a war film or the news, so I would look away for the latter. If it was a whole programme I found undesirable I could read, and I too would wear headphones and listen to Classic FM. What I was sad about were the times when we were both happily viewing the same thing, but he would still wear headphones. To enhance the quality of music listening for a musician I could understand, but these were just normal films or programmes. The message I picked up was 'Don't talk to me; I want to be in my own world without you intruding.' It's not as if I was one of those annoying people who keep chatting or making comments about a film when you want to get absorbed in it. The frequent wearing of headphones was an early sign that Gerry was beginning to withdraw from me. It's a bit like the way he rarely wanted to converse on a car journey, like my close friend's husband; and started walking ahead of me, rather than beside me, when we went out anywhere.

Gerry was very ambivalent about company anyway. I've already mentioned his need for lots of solitude, which I think I respected sufficiently. It was very rare indeed for him to sit in the lounge with me or any visiting friends or relations just conversing. If nothing was available for viewing, he would take himself off upstairs to his workspace for long periods, even if it was his own relatives who were staying with us for a few days. (He would do the same with all the Bank Holidays even at Christmas time, making them just like a normal day, from choice.) He wasn't overly thrilled about family (or anybody's) visits, but aside from this feeling about not really having a connection with his own, he didn't really find them unpleasant. He just didn't want to be around for the chatting. He would come along on day trips and of course be with us for mealtimes, except breakfast, but make himself scarce at the first opportunity, leaving me to entertain his family. Fortunately I got on well with all the ones who came to stay, and indeed was very fond of them. His sister and husband are still frequently in touch with me, which gives me pleasure.

As regards breakfast, I once said to Gerry that I would love it if, just one day a week of his choice, we could both go down to have breakfast together instead of his going directly to his office to check emails as soon as he was dressed, every single day. He was totally unwilling to make this concession. The other day my closest friend asked me how he had been about routines being broken, as she has another friend with an adult son with AS. I reflected and thought of this example where he was, I guess, totally dismayed at the thought of altering his daily pattern. I did manage to get him to agree to sitting at a table for each Sunday lunch, which I always tried to make a very special meal; but I know it was a grudging assent, especially if he would have preferred to watch an action film while eating. Similarly, I learned soon after we got together that I had better not suggest a more convenient way to drive to places in our town that I knew so well, as he was totally resistant to this, with the consequence that once or twice we nearly missed a train due to traffic hold-ups that I was planning to avoid by a clearer route.

Basically Gerry seemed to bristle about anything that seemed to be 'expected' of him by anybody and he would retreat from it. He resisted all kinds of constraints, restrictions, guidelines and feedback. I have mentioned his tremendous skills in journalism, and the programme notes he wrote for concerts were always very lively and entertaining. As the print deadline approached, though, he would get exasperated by anyone pushing him to provide the copy and always left it to the very last possible minute, or even just after, to people's intense annoyance. I suspect the same was sometimes true for the school reports; but any Head of Department or School Secretary would tell you that goes with the territory, I guess. Nothing unusual there! I know that the ending of his favourite conducting job – well after he'd left me – came about, among several other reasons, because he refused to start rehearsals promptly despite always arriving in plenty of time. Another big factor in the loss of that post was his unwillingness to heed hints given by the committee that there was growing dissatisfaction about his manner during those sessions.

People were beginning to leave the choir in ones and twos so that, over time the numbers dwindled by a third. They would usually give Gerry plausible reasons for going, such as pressure of other commitments, to spare his feelings. What they told the committee was very different: that to begin with they found some of his jokes and teasing and disdain for political correctness mildly amusing, but that eventually it began to pall, or even feel like bullying if the same choir members were the butt of the teasing or jocular complaints time after time. He certainly has enthusiasm, sometimes exuberance and a magnetic personality and many have liked him very much, perhaps for quite a long time. Sad to say that over and over again, with his challenges over what making good lasting friendships requires, he ends up regarding some of those people as enemies. Recently the former 'best friend' remarked to me: "So much for twenty-seven years of friendship!", now that she and her husband have been cast aside.

As he seems to have changed so much in the last few years, she also asked me if I thought I'd had a 'civilising influence' over him during our time together, since he'd been much more inclined to be co-operative with the committee in the first six or seven years of conducting the choir. I had to think about that one and ponder the root meaning of 'civilise'. What I had tried to offer was the 'kindly and gently' pointing out of likely outcomes that I referred to in the Introduction. Sometimes he found that acceptable and so it was well received, and sometimes not. It probably backfired on me later under the label 'patronising behaviour.' Apparently being 'civilised' is acting in the manner befitting a citizen (for which I think we can read 'member of any community') and being courteous. The paradox for this particular Aspie, and probably many others, is that on the one hand he himself was exceedingly sensitive, with a quick reaction of feeling hurt, misunderstood or unjustly criticised; but, on the other hand, very often utterly unable to be sensitive to the feelings of others. Hence his coming across as 'inconsiderate' as I referred to in chapter six.

Part of his own hyper-sensitivity, I think, was this impression he'd picked up in childhood and teens of always 'being in the wrong.' A little aside here, which I've thought of because some people got the idea he thinks rather a lot of himself; (I see it as over-compensation for low self-esteem). If that meant they saw him as 'big-headed' they were literally right; and until reading

Tony Attwood's book I had no idea that many people with Asperger Syndrome do literally have a much larger skull size than average. It took us years and years to find him one of the broad-brimmed rain hats that would be big enough for him, and then only because just one of several XXL models in the shop had been made slightly ampler than the others! It gave me enormous joy to buy it for him and see the delight on his face.

Chapter Ten

TREAD SOFTLY…
(FOR YOU TREAD ON MY DREAMS)

I once said to Gerry: "I'm the realist in this partnership; you're the dreamer!" I guess I shouldn't have been surprised that he took this as a criticism. It wasn't meant to be; I was just reminding him that, since we had quite contrasting approaches to life, and especially the management of money, we needed to negotiate compromises when we each had different plans and schemes. Having observed a large number of couples of friends over many years (most of whom, I'm happy to say, have sustained marriages for decades, apparently happily) I realise that it's often quite beneficial if the two individuals are not too similar in outlook. I know that Gerry's bringing more spontaneity into my life was a refreshing change, and that my ability to plan and budget – for instance – enabled us to stay in our three-storey four-bedroom Victorian semi-detached house with the flatlet he used as work premises, living comfortably enough and usually managing an annual holiday, for our seventeen years together, despite our relatively modest incomes.

One cherished dream he had from the outset, and probably also before I met him, was of winning the lottery. I sometimes wonder what would have become of him, or us, if he had become a millionaire. I don't take an optimistic view of that remote possibility. I reminded him once that a lot of our visibly happiest occasions were during years when money was in short supply. But because we were very close and could go and enjoy low-cost days out, perhaps with a picnic, we had wonderful times, as he frequently said without being asked. I remember the first time he sent me flowers, ordered over the telephone and delivered to me at work. At the time he still had a large amount of debt, so the common sense part of me considered (very briefly) thanking him, but saying that I knew he loved me dearly and so he didn't need to make extravagant gestures. I soon realised that this would have seemed like a rejection and, as I adored being given flowers, I just told him how thrilled I was. He always said: "What did (various named colleagues) say?" I think I mainly replied that they seemed very envious, as indeed they often were in those early years whenever they saw him making a huge fuss of me, all smiles and enthusiasm and bounce. What they tended to say was: "It's not your anniversary … or your birthday; is he trying to make up after a row?" It was never that; just his magnificent loving gesture, and an element of wanting to show it to others; because I don't think he ever had any flowers delivered to the house for me! Apart from the anniversary bouquets, which were lovely, much appreciated and much thanked-for, I later on needed to content myself (like lots of women who love being given flowers) with a bunch picked up at the garage or the supermarket! What a demanding so-and-so I am! I told you before: just human!

Gerry's generosity also extended to charity subscription canvassers in the street. They are not seen so much these days; but

I was very touched when Gerry signed up for the first two or three of these, and the fact that he always bought *The Big Issue* and had a bit of a chat with the sellers. Once I realised that he was going to sign up indiscriminately for a monthly donation to every single charity that approached him I felt I had to say something to make him think it over, especially at a time when I was still helping substantially, both to pay off his credit card debts and asking for only a very modest contribution to our home expenses, until he got steadier and more remunerative work. One of his sisters-in-law, on the first time of meeting me, made a scathing comment – only half under her breath – saying: "Gerry always manages to find a woman who will provide a home for him." I felt just as indignant about this humiliating comment in front of several other members of his family as I had done when his lovely mother – and I really mean that – asked me on the phone after our first few months together: "And is he paying his way?" I lied that he was! Despite my loyal defensiveness over this issue, they were only speaking of him based on past experience. Mother-in-law also asked ever so many times on the phone: "Everything still alright?" I only found out very recently that his family had never known how or why Gerry's first marriage, and the following twelve-year life partnership he was in before he came to me, had ended.

A propos of his sister-in-law's remark re women providing homes for Gerry, I'd always found it very amusing that after our first 'date', when he visited me for almost twenty-four hours, he'd stood on the pavement opposite as I waved goodbye from my front step, looked across at the handsome house where I lived and asked: "Is this your house, or do you rent it?" A few people have thought that a preposterous thing to ask, and consider that I should have heard an alarm bell with that enquiry. It all makes complete sense to me now; but after I'd laughingly quoted that remark to one or two close friends who visited us, Gerry told me he didn't want me to say it any more, so I respected his wishes. Teasing never went down well, and indeed was often not recognised as such. Incidentally, in a state of stunned shock in 2013, as he told me he'd be leaving me fourteen hours later to move in with the lover he'd had during his first marriage, thirty-odd years earlier, I remarked sardonically: "I hope you didn't ask her if she owned her flat!", to which he replied, deadpan: "I didn't need to; she volunteered the information."

I suppose another indicator of lack of realism is a certain degree of gullibility. I listened in horror one day when we were in the lounge and Gerry picked up a phone call purporting to be from his bank. Within no time I heard him giving full information on his account and personal details. I started gesticulating warnings to him as he was speaking but that achieved nothing; and when he finished the call his face was like thunder, and he told me off for interfering. He then stomped up to his office, leaving me to ponder for a few minutes what to do next, for the best. I took a deep breath, followed him upstairs, knocked on his office door (I always did) and said: "I'm sorry that what I did really annoyed you, but just for my peace of mind would you please go on line and type in the phone number the bank gave you to contact them?" With a huge sigh he complied and then looked rather crestfallen. He immediately phoned the fraud line at his bank, having seen that the number he'd been given was indeed associated with a scam. I didn't expect any apology, or even to hear: "You were right!" – and I was not mistaken. The other day my friend who's married to an Aspie, whom she also seems to adore, said of her husband: "Oh, he <u>never</u> apologises; that would be admitting he was wrong."

In the few years before he left me Gerry became increasingly focussed on obtaining the wherewithal to achieve his long-cherished dreams. After all, the American 'spiritual' programme which he had begun to read avidly in 2011, spending ever-increasing amounts of time listening to the CDs and on-line teaching associated with it, promised on its website's home page *'the fulfilment of all your Life's dreams.'* This was music to Gerry's ears; or should I say a delight to his eyes. Around that time he came across another couple of schemes that he was really keen to subscribe to. One was guaranteeing huge amounts of income for no effort, just acting as a link person for something. I happened to knock at the door of his office and go in to say that lunch was ready, just as he was discovering that, though he'd only had to pay £10 to pass the first hurdle of signing up, at each subsequent stage he was being asked to pay ever-increasing amounts. Another website he was thrilled about invited him to sign up, pay a fee, and he would be given some magic numbers. Provided he used them in the way prescribed and did the correct thing with a sort of talisman, a vast amount of money was sure to arrive within a specified number of days. I think he is still waiting (or I could cynically say, it just occurs to me, that it was hugely delayed and took the form of the post-divorce financial settlement he received as a share of the house that had been solely in my name!).

Before I go into what those most important of his dreams were and how he set off in pursuit of them, I'd like to ponder what I think I'd have tried to do differently if I'd known through our years together what I know now. That may seem a futile exercise to some. ("Water under the bridge." "Too late now." "No point having regrets." "Life moves on." "You'll never know if it would have made any difference." "Put it down to experience." "You did the best you could under the circumstances." "Hindsight is a wonderful thing!" "It wasn't your fault." "Nothing can be done about it.") I'm well aware that all these clichés and platitudes have some truth in them. In Joan and Miroslav Borysenko's excellent book *The Power of the Mind to Heal*, which I have found a great support over recent months, there is a quotation from G.K.Chesterton which I find very meaningful – especially when I consider well-meaning, but to me irritating, urges from people to 'move on': *'Real development is not leaving things behind, as on a road, but drawing life from them, as from a root.'*

The hope I expressed earlier in this book was that one or two people might perhaps manage to pick up some hints and thus avoid the heartache and pain of loss that I still feel; though memories of our exceedingly happy times far outweigh times thinking of the agonising closing months of our married life together. When Gerry had finally agreed, reluctantly, that we would try and talk over why he had grown away from me (talking about any problem was against the teaching of his spiritual programme), I remarked late one night in bed, when he expressed appreciation of my physical affection at that point: "This all should have been repaired!" He said: "Could we still?" I said: "Let me know when you want to talk about that tomorrow". Two days passed, and I reminded him, saying: "So have you anything new to bring to the table?" He replied: "I've only myself to bring." I was – gently – at the end of my tether by then. But I now find those words so touching. I understand so much more about AS. His words were the truth! He also said around this time: "Whatever it is you want me to do or be, I either can't or am not." In fact I just wanted <u>some</u> attention and voluntary affection on a regular basis, as I'd had for the first fifteen years.

In no particular order I'd like to have **tried** some of the following ways of coping, reacting or responding:

I would accept that my values (e.g. about care for the environment) are for me, but not for me to try and inculcate in a partner. Apparently the root meaning of that word is to trample, which does not seem good! Instilling, i.e. adding drop by drop, would be better. But even so, he needs to express who <u>he</u> is, not who I am.

I wouldn't try to give him advice on healthy eating, the unhealthy aspects of his mild addiction and preventative health generally. These were intended to benefit him; but they were also based on my fear of losing him to an earlier death than was to be hoped. I thereby may have seemed to be impinging on his freedoms.

If I thought something was 'up' with him, I wouldn't say: "Is anything wrong?" I'd try instead: "Is there anything you need from me just now?" There was a time he came in simply saying: "I'm not a very nice person." He may have been feeling he wanted to admit something to me, but instead of making space for this I immediately reassured him that he was a <u>lovely</u> person and that I loved him very much. If, for once, he was wanting to reveal some of his innermost turmoil I may have blocked that process in my haste to 'make him feel better'. This is something 'Rescuers' do regularly, and though I think I'm less of a rescuer than I was in my late thirties, some of us do tend to retain these tendencies.

I honestly can't think of how I might have approached the communication challenges more effectively. I considered that the Couple Meetings that I suggested had a good format and seemed to work pretty well. I thought that arranging for each of us to take turns in speaking first at a given session, mirroring back – after uninterrupted listening – what each thought the other had said for the sake of clarity, and each making reminder notes that we also read back, made for open and honest sharing that took into account the vulnerabilities of each of us. Neuro-typical partners have emotional wounds and needs too!

The next 'Wish I'd…' may seem an odd one, as it's purely a hunch. I gave up sleeping in my birthday suit after I passed the menopause because I felt more comfortable and less overheated with a layer of cotton round me. I genuinely think that our physical and emotional bonding was lessened by this and in that mythical land of 'if I had my time over again' I'd put up with feeling sticky for the joy of not having to request the cuddling that had always been so freely and eagerly given. Skin-to-skin may affect bonding well beyond infancy.

If I thought a dream of Gerry's that was verbalised was 'beyond hope', I like to think I'd say something along the lines of: "So what would need to happen for us to reach that, and what would be a first step?" We did try to get that bigger house in a county where they were cheaper, but ours didn't sell before the dream home we'd found was sold. I was up for that challenge aged about fifty-three, but not at sixty-five when I'd had ample opportunity to see Gerry's pattern of work situations. He'd twice started training courses that could well have led to good musical opportunities which might have brought him the sort of income he said he'd like (in 2012 he'd mentioned £30,000 as a desired annual salary); but he'd never completed either of them.

Perhaps most importantly of all I would realise that what is not seen as 'spiritual' to one person may well, and indeed does, seem so to others. We cannot really take another by the hand and lead him or her down a similar spiritual path to the one we are on, since that journey above all others is the one that must be self-chosen and followed wherever it may lead. Any lessons we take from life experiences are solely our own. It is vitally important to respect what it is that calls out to a partner in that realm of being and not to make disparaging remarks about it. My fear of losing him to that spiritual programme, and therefore probably to any seemingly suitable woman who also followed it, put me into panic mode and I consider I handled this in a most unhelpful way. And I can forgive myself for that wholly natural reaction!

Gerry wrote down, as the dreams of what he wanted to receive: "More money; a bigger house; a perfect relationship, one that meets all my needs at all levels; more success with my music; more high-profile well-paid gigs…" Most of these were material goals, therefore one reason why I found it difficult to see the pursuit of these in the context of a 'spiritual programme' – though I'd been well aware over many years of my life, in a somewhat 'alternative' scene, of 'prosperity consciousness' teaching. Although these mainly material goals do not yet seem to have 'manifested' for him, (though of course I can't know about the quality of his current marriage), I think I can nevertheless see what this spiritual (mainly on-line) community offered him, that he has always yearned for. One is a sense of not just being 'ok' – which I guess he had never truly felt – but of receiving constantly positive 'strokes'; that he is a wonderful person and indeed perfect, just as he is. And when members of the community do gather together in the flesh for their retreats he can go deep and feel, for however short a time, a cathartic and deeply moving sense of **connection**, not only with his fellow devotees, but with the Divine source of all that is. That is bound to feel wonderful, and all the more so for a person who finds experiencing a true sense of connection with fellow-humans so hard to reach and sustain. I read some of the writing of Dr. Jonice Webb (which I first discovered on a website called *Psychcentral.com*) re a sense of not having one's emotional needs sufficiently met in childhood. She states: "*Having your feelings walled off is basically a recipe for feeling disconnected and unfulfilled in your adult life. It makes emotions puzzling…*". I truly believe I did the best I could to meet the challenges of a neuro-diverse marriage, without any knowledge that that was what I was in, and without the benefit of any guidance other than from my own intuition. So I did not believe, as one person gently suggested, that Gerry may have turned to this programme because of dissatisfaction in our marriage. I believe it came out of a much deeper and more fundamental soul-yearning. He had sought his 'soul-mate' from his teens, he told me. But perhaps, in reality, our only soul-mate – who will never disappoint us, never let us down, criticise or judge us, always understand and accept us – is the ever-perfectly-loving Source of our being. I hope Gerry will always be able to rest in those everlasting arms.

ACKNOWLEDGEMENTS

First and foremost I express my profound gratitude for the wonderful happiness brought to me by Gerry for full fifteen years. I would not have missed them for the world.

Next, thanks to my dear friend of well over twenty years, Patricia Corner, for unfailing encouragement, love and company. We were friends 'BG' (before Gerry came into my life!) but since he left, words cannot adequately express my appreciation of her faithful support and loyalty. Without that, I am not sure how I would have come through. All her privileged friends know that hers is an exceptionally caring nature.

I am grateful, too, to the expert in the field of AS who has given me much support and clear encouragement to publish – she knows who she is! – and thanks to my patient proof-reader and friend Ellyn.

Last, but by no means least I thank all at Aspect Design for their expertise and exceptional service.

RECOMMENDED READING

Asperger's Syndrome – A Guide for Parents and Professionals
    Tony Attwood
    pub. Jessica Kingsley 1998
    (Please note: this was the only book on the subject that I had read before writing my own, as I didn't want mine to be in any way derivative.)

The other half of Asperger Syndrome
    Maxine C. Aston
    pub. National Autistic Society 2001

Aspergers in Love
    Maxine C. Aston
    pub. Jessica Kingsley 2003

Asperger Syndrome and Long-term relationships
    Ashley Stanford
    pub. Jessica Kingsley 2003

Marriage and Lasting relationships with Asperger's Syndrome
    Eva A. Mendes
    pub. Jessica Kingsley 2015

Our socially awkward marriage
    Tom Peters and Linda Peters
    pub. Brookside Press 2016
    (Short stories about the authors' life together, with delightful humour at times.)